6-15-53

GUIDING WORKERS *in* CHRISTIAN EDUCATION

THE COOPERATIVE SERIES

LEADERSHIP TRAINING TEXTBOOKS

Many thousands of lay workers in Protestant churches attend interdenominational leadership education schools each year. It is essential that the courses offered and the text materials used be acceptable to the many varieties of Protestant groups found in our American communities.

The Cooperative Series of leadership training textbooks are produced to meet that need. They are planned by the Division of Christian Education of the National Council of the Churches of Christ in the U.S.A., representing thirty-nine Protestant denominations. The Cooperative Publication Association, an interdenominational group of denominational editors and publishers, selects the writers and provides editorial supervision to insure sound educational values, practical usefulness, and interdenominational approval and acceptance.

Guiding Workers *in* Christian Education

FRANK M. McKIBBEN

PUBLISHED FOR
The Cooperative Publication Association
by
ABINGDON-COKESBURY PRESS
New York • Nashville

GUIDING WORKERS IN CHRISTIAN EDUCATION

Library of Congress Catalog Card Number: 53-5397

PRINTED IN THE UNITED STATES OF AMERICA

CONTENTS

I. Christian Education Can Be Improved . . 7

II. Who Will Guide Improvement? 15

III. Conditions Essential to Effective Education 37

IV. Developing Common Understandings . . 59

V. Guidance Through Group Activity . . . 78

VI. Guiding Individual Workers 98

VII. Developing Competent Creative Workers . 115

VIII. How Effective Is Christian Education? . 135

Selected Bibliography 158

CHAPTER ONE

Christian Education Can Be Improved

MRS. JONES, teacher of the third-grade junior boys, was studying the lessons for the next few Sundays. There were many things about them she did not understand. There seemed to be plenty of material. In fact, she felt there was too much. How could she use all of it in the time available? Several plans for its use were suggested in the teacher's manual. Which plan should she follow? Her thought shifted to one of her boys—Fred. What was the reason for his continued disinterest and failure to respond? How could she interest him in the work of the class? What could be done to lessen the noise and confusion that surrounded her pupils as they met? These and other problems troubled Mrs. Jones. Where could she get help? If only there were a helping teacher! Or if her superintendent would counsel with her more. Mrs. Jones felt sorely in need of assistance.

The Genius of Protestant Education. Mrs. Jones is doubtless typical of many among the hundreds of thousands of people serving in the educational work of Protestant churches, as teachers, counselors of youth, superintendents of departments, music directors, home visitors, secretaries, recreational leaders, and officers of various organizations. Protestant churches have committed the formal education of their young to this vast army of volunteer workers. An increasing number of them have a measure of training, and many are qualified by experience; but the great majority of them are without specific training or experience for their important work. One of the truly remarkable things about the church's program of religious education from its very beginning in this country has been the devoted leadership of the great body of laymen and laywomen who year after year have responded to the call to service. While the quality of Christian education has at times been tragically poor, its vitality has been demonstrated over and over again by the participation of these millions of lay people. Surely there is an unconscious genius about it. Perhaps this is due to its similarity to the manner in which Jesus, the master teacher, went about his mission. We never cease to wonder over his selection of twelve ordinary, untutored men to be his disciples. We marvel at his willingness to entrust to them the redemptive work he had initiated. He had great confidence in and held high hopes for average persons such as made up the small company of common people who under the inspiration of his personality and teachings, and guided by the Holy Spirit, helped form the Christian Church.

Protestant churches have established a seemingly permanent pattern of education, that of a Sunday church school, using volunteer workers. This session is supplemented by study, fellowship, worship and service groups meeting at other times on Sunday and through the week. There has been a great increase in the number of men and women entering the work of Christian education as professionally trained ministers, directors of religious education, youth counselors, and supervisors in the local church. Still the Sunday morning and evening sessions continue to constitute the major program. It is largely in the hands of lay people. These volunteer workers have done noble service. However, with each succeeding year more concern is felt over providing better training and more effective assistance to these workers.

The Crying Need for Improvement. The great need of the present moment is for the improvement of the Christian nurture provided for all ages in the church. The church school has been and still is the greatest single recruiting and evangelizing force in the church. Seven out of ten of the new members entering the church come through the church school. Often, however, there is greater zeal to increase the enrollment and attendance than to improve the quality of the nurture provided for those who attend. The Sunday church school, limited in time and poor in quality as it often is, represents the major means, aside from the home, for providing religious nurture for the vast majority of the children, youth, and adults in Protestant churches. This fact alone should inspire strenuous efforts to make such training as effective as possible. The future of the church, and more important still, of Christianity itself, depends more than is realized upon the quality of the religious nurture provided through the church school. *To provide such training is the first task of the Christian church. To aid in its accomplishment is the major concern of all workers in Christian education.* In working at this task we are fulfilling the final and supreme injunction of the Master, "Go . . . teach . . . ." And in every effort to develop capable, devoted Christians we may feel that we are truly co-workers with God.

Competition Is Keen. The church is confronted with strong competition in gaining the response of those to whom it is seeking to minister. The quality of public education is being constantly improved. The appeal of commercialized entertainment is growing stronger every year. Recreational and service agencies in local communities are increasingly calling for the time, energy, and loyalty of young and old alike. The church faces keen competition on all sides. Many of these competing activities are highly beneficial. But they challenge the time, energy, talents, and loyalties of multitudes of people. In that sense they are in competition with the church. The church may meet this competition successfully only if it makes the call to Christian discipleship clear and compelling, and if it greatly improves the quality of its program. The crying need of the hour is for *improvement*—the broadening, enriching, and strengthening of the church's total educational program.

Christian Education Can Be Improved. In the face of these needs it is most encouraging to realize that there can be immediate and significant improvement of Christian education. During the past few years an amazing amount of guidance and resource material has become available to workers in the local church. The various denominations, working individually and co-operatively, have developed vital materials and comprehensive programs. These have much in common and have grown out of the best thinking of scores of trained leaders. They reflect the wide and varied experiences of those who have attempted to chart the course of Christian education for the Protestant churches. These blueprints or standards are available to church workers anywhere in America and in all denominations. In addition rich resources in the form of program suggestions, leaders' guides, standards, varied curriculums, and teacher-training aids are readily accessible. Never before in the history of religious education has such assistance in the form of program suggestions and materials been offered to the local church in the development and improvement of Christian education.

In addition increasing numbers of ministers are receiving training in guiding and supervising the education programs of their churches. Many churches are able to command the services of professionally trained full-time directors of religious education. Denominations, singly and in co-operation, are employing men and women to serve full time in various phases of supervisory educational leadership in states, communities, conferences, synods, and districts. Their primary responsibility is to give assistance to workers in local churches. Thus on every hand improvement measures are available. There would seem to be little excuse for any worker or group of workers failing to bring about improvement in the quality of the educational work in the local church.

Improvement Calls for Supervision. There is nothing mysterious about improvement. It calls for analysis, evaluation, and experimental procedures. We have much of the "know-how" of improvement. There is much about effective Christian nurture, it is true, that still remains unknown; but we have gained valuable insights and experience during the past quarter century as the modern program of religious education has developed. Public schools and character-education agencies have been steadily at work with professionally trained leaders in efforts to improve the quality of their programs. Practically all their findings are available to those working in Christian education. Improvement procedures consist largely of analysis of the various program activities into their detailed particulars. Careful study of the kinds of responses secured from individuals participating in them is required. Understanding of each phase of the program and of the objectives of each particular session is essential. An evaluative attitude must be maintained at all times.

The various procedures that make for improvement may be described under the term "supervision." This is a relatively new term in Christian education. It has long been in use in public education. It is simply a technical term embracing all those activities engaged in by individuals attempting to bring about improvement. These procedures include the development of common understandings of basic interpretations of Christian education, joint study of problems, setting up objectives and their constant refinement, co-operative program building, guidance of individuals in their work, the use of evaluation schedules, the direction of group study and activity, visitation and follow-up conferences, plans for demonstration teaching, providing teacher-training classes, development of library and resource materials, making surveys, the use of records, understanding and use of appropriate curriculum materials, the use of tests, preparation of mimeograph instructions, individual and group evaluations, and many similar activities.

The Purposes of Supervision. The purposes of supervision may be stated as follows:

1. To guide those responsible for Christian education in studying the total program as it is being provided in the light of the most representative standards of their denomination and of Protestantism in general;

2. To lead workers into a fuller understanding of the nature and meaning of Christian nurture and of the conditions necessary for its fullest realization;

3. To aid workers in the various aspects of the program to determine the objectives they may seek in their work and to help them discover the extent to which they are being achieved;

4. To develop among teachers and leaders a willingness and ability to analyze and objectively to evaluate the procedures and materials they are using with a view to determining the elements of strength and weakness and to undertake specific measures of improvement;

5. To develop schedules and measuring instruments by which the program may be more accurately evaluated and to train workers in their use;

6. To carry forward continuously a program of enlistment, motivation, training, and placement in service of men and women who will be needed to carry forward the total program;

7. To help educate the parents and total constituency of the church in the necessity and importance of Christian education and to encourage and provide for their active participation in and support of the program.

The chapters of this book will deal in some detail with the more important considerations and procedures which will aid and encourage those responsible for securing improvement. The treatment is necessarily brief owing to limitations of space, but it is hoped that it is sufficient to provide substantial assistance. Those who are in any way responsible for building and improving the program are encouraged to study the chapters that follow to become familiar with the principles and procedures of effective supervision. To those with experience and training these suggestions may seem quite well known and fairly widely used. Yet they are those that have grown out of experience and should be universally employed if improvement is to be achieved. To those with limited training and experience the procedures suggested may seem difficult to follow, yet the simpler supervisory activities can be employed by anyone willing to give time and study to the various chapters, and who will engage in program building, evaluation, and study of the various elements entering into effective Christian nurture. Most of us will need to begin where we are in preparation, experience, and opportunity and move from there into better understanding and more effective leadership. We must ever remember that we "learn to teach by teaching." Likewise we will become proficient in supervision by actually engaging in supervisory activities.

The procedures of improvement are definitely evangelistic in nature. We are confronted with serious losses from the church and by the recognized ineffectiveness of many aspects of Christian education. It may readily be seen that if by more careful follow-up of pupils, or by some measure of improvement in teaching or counseling, a child, youth, or adult is actually "saved" to Christian discipleship, such improvement is definitely evangelistic in nature. Only such a passion to "save" and "hold" people, young and old, will motivate church workers to initiate the vigorous measures of improvement of Christian education needed in most churches.

Some of the keenest satisfactions to be experienced by teachers, officers, committee members, and others serving in Christian education will be the realization that the program is being constantly improved, that results are being more fully achieved. It may be observed in the more enthusiastic response of pupils to class activities, in the more meaningful participation of individuals in group worship, in deeper commitment to Christ on the part of church members, in growing skill in applying Christian teachings to everyday living, and in more rewarding, enriching fellowship within the community of believers. They are satisfactions worth striving for.

For Further Study

1. To what degree is the point of view regarding Christian education presented in this chapter accepted in your church? How would you seek to bring about better understanding and fuller appreciation of Christian education?
2. What elements of (1) greatest effectiveness and (2) marked weakness do you observe in the educational program of your church?
3. To what extent is there awareness of the necessity of improvement among your workers? How would you proceed to arouse concern over the quality of the program?
4. To what extent are the many and varied available resources in Christian education being used in your church?

CHAPTER TWO

Who Will Guide Improvement?

THE IMPROVEMENT of the local program of Christian education is the concern of all who are in any way identified with it. Such efforts to bring about improvement will involve many people. Those efforts will be most successful that in the end enlist the participation of a large number of persons. It is necessary of course to assign responsibility in supervision and to discover and secure the services of those qualified to direct improvement procedures. Such work will certainly call for the investment of time. In most cases it will require special training on the part of those who supervise. The discovery of such personnel in most churches will be a new experience, for the great majority of churches have not emphasized this form of service. In some churches it will involve bringing in a professionally trained leader. In an increasing number of churches the minister will assume at least some responsibility for supervision for the reason that many ministers are receiving definite training in directing the program of Christian education. This is true also because the minister is usually the only person in the local church giving full time to Christian service.

In all likelihood it may mean simply the selection of one or more members of the local staff to undertake this specific responsibility. Who are the most likely persons in the average church? Certainly the following would be among those who may be considered for supervisory work: the general superintendent, the divisional or departmental superintendent, a special supervisor or helping teacher, the chairman or a committee of the board of Christian education,[1] the director of Christian education or the minister.

The Superintendent as Supervisor. The work of the superintendent is usually thought of as being administrative. He is responsible under the guidance of the board of Christian education for setting up the organization and personnel of the educational program, especially that which comes under the term "church school." His office is ordinarily concerned with:

1. Getting the program organized and in operation
2. Seeing that personnel is provided
3. Securing properly selected and approved curriculum material and supplies
4. Making sure that groups are properly placed and that adequate equipment is provided
5. Planning workers' conferences and other staff meetings
6. Planning for keeping accurate and full records
7. Interpreting the program to the officials of the church and securing moral and financial support from the constituency
8. Seeing that other requirements for educational work are met

He will frequently be assisted in these duties by one or several persons, such as an assistant, departmental leaders, a secretary, a supply officer, a treasurer, and other officers of the board of

[1] Various terms are used among the different denominations and local churches to designate the body responsible for the educational program of the local church: church board of education, committee on religious education or Christian, or Commission on religious education. For the sake of simplicity and uniformity one term is used throughout this book in referring to such a group. Whenever the term "board of Christian education" is used, it will be understood that it refers to the same group that may be called by a different title in some denominations and churches.

Christian education. Such a group of persons, small or large, may constitute a part of the supervisory staff.

Practically everything the superintendent does has a bearing on the effectiveness of Christian education. Good administration means better work throughout the program. Most superintendents do not attempt supervision in the sense that is discussed in this book because they have not been led to see their work in this relation, also because most of them have had at best limited training for that kind of leadership. Yet really significant opportunities are open to any superintendent who earnestly desires to help bring about improvement. He needs to become keenly aware of these kinds of services, commit himself to working persistently at them, and endeavor to prepare himself in every way possible for such leadership. A number of ways in which the superintendent may participate in the supervision of Christian education will be discussed briefly in the hope of guiding superintendents in this form of service.

Improvement Opportunities for the Superintendent. All educational activity is set in some kind of organizational framework. The very manner in which people are brought together in the various relationships and activities constitutes a vital part of the educational process itself. Organization brings about functional groupings; it assigns responsibility; it arranges for widespread particiation; it assembles and releases resources; it provides social contacts and promotes fellowship, and thus plays an important role in the development of individuals and groups. The superintendent who understands the educational values in organizational procedures will be constantly seeking to make organizations serve the ends of effective Christian education.

The manner in which pupil records are kept will have great significance for the effectiveness of the program. (This will be discussed in Chapter III.) Scores of churches have had very inadequate and carelessly kept record systems. Serious losses from the life of the church and the work of the church school frequently occur largely because no one misses pupils when they are absent or leave. There is no adequate follow-up, and little information is secured about pupils for the permanent files. There is increasing recognition in church work of the importance of properly kept data regarding every person participating in any way in the life and work of the fellowship. As more extended pastoral care, counseling, and teacher-pupil fellowship become a part of the program, carefully kept records of whatever data are regarded as essential will prove of inestimable value. Genuine understanding and concern with respect to the record system and skill in making such information available to the working staff will enable the superintendent to render a real contribution to the effectiveness of the program. He may not be directly responsible for records, yet he will be in a position greatly to influence policies and procedures.

The church-school superintendent usually assumes considerable responsibility for securing and placing officers, teachers, and counselors for the program. Here again he plays an important role in determining the quality of the work done. He helps materially to secure a better type of work throughout the program when he (1) discovers and enlists promising and capable people, (2) places them at strategic places in the program, (3) motivates them to do their best, (4) provides training opportunities for them, (5) engenders devotion and enthusiasm among them, (6) promotes teamwork, and (7) sees to it that their services are appreciated. Others will undoubtedly be working with the superintendent and possibly will carry the major responsibility in the field of leadership, yet many of these opportunities for supervisory service will be his. To what extent he will attempt to work with small groups in the detailed planning of the program or in counseling individual teachers in their work, or will enter into the more technical aspects of the program will depend largely upon the inclination, training, and time of the individual superintendent. Certainly he who attempts these important forms of leadership will need to enter upon a real program of training.

The superintendent may help to interpret to other official groups and to the constituency of the church the nature and needs of the program, the special emphasis being carried forward, and the financial and personnel requirements. Often the superintendent is a lay person of wide acquaintance and high standing in the church. He has an influential voice in the councils of the fellowship. He opens up opportunities for educating various people regarding the program. Even where there is a professional director of religious education, the superintendent may render invaluable service.

While the general superintendent may lack extended training for supervisory leadership, it is entirely possible that he will possess certain special insights and skills. He may be able to secure loyalty and enthusiasm among his fellow workers that will be reflected in more faithful and skillful service. There is increasing recognition of the importance of establishing helpful, wholesome relations among people, especially those who work together at a common task. This is sometimes called "morale," "esprit de corps," or "fellowship." The general superintendent stands in a unique position to help create such a spirit among the workers in the educational program, within the board of Christian education, among the members of the council of church workers, within the departmental staff, and among the pupils of the church school. Sometimes such morale or fellowship seems to develop naturally. More often it is something that must be cultivated. The superintendent who takes seriously the building of such relationships will study the different ways in which people may be brought together and as a result may enter into rewarding associations and activities. He will become something of a "social engineer."

The superintendent may be a businessman with keen interest in and some ability with records and reports. He may be able "to make figures talk." Statistics instead of being dead and uninteresting may be made to keep all concerned informed and stimulated by what they reveal about the success or failure of the program. Or the superintendent may possess natural ability to counsel with individual workers. He may not always have the insights that will enable him to advise on some of the more technical aspects of the work, but he can be a sympathetic listener and give much help and inspiration to workers in need. He may possess genuine insights into the general strategy of Christian education and be able to interpret needs and opportunities in this field to official groups and to the entire constituency in the church in a way no other person can. Or again, he may have interest in the handling of housing and equipment. By a study of standards in this field he might become able to render a special contribution to the effectiveness of the work of his associates through improving the physical conditions affecting their leadership. He may well study the chapters that follow to discover the supervisory activities he may wish to engage in or prepare himself to do. The various supervisory activities taken up in the following chapters are treated in an over-all manner, with the idea that the supervisor, whether the volunteer part-time worker or the full-time professionally trained leader, will engage in these activities in whatever way may be possible or seem wise. There are numerous pieces of literature available from the headquarters of the various denominations and the National Council of Churches designed to aid the superintendent in understanding his opportunities and in meeting them. He should be sure to secure these materials.

Whoever the supervisor may be, one thing is highly essential.

Such a person must be able to establish rapport with those with whom he works. One of the most important conditions of good supervisory leadership is effective working relationships with the individual teacher, the department staff, the pupils, and the supporting constituency. Unless the supervisor has had unusual experience or has unique native abilities, he will find it necessary to undertake seriously the study of group relationships and activities. The more professional aspects of this problem are represented in the term "group dynamics." The matter of working with groups is taken up in detail in Chapter V. It is mentioned here as one of the qualifications of supervisory personnel.

The Departmental Superintendent as Supervisor. One of the most natural persons to look to for supervisory leadership will be the departmental superintendent. There are a number of reasons for this. Such a superintendent deals with a limited part of the program. He thereby sustains a close relation to all that goes on. Usually the departmental superintendent has had a part in the selection of the teachers and other workers in the department and often holds them to the work with a strong personal loyalty. Such a superintendent is responsible as no one else is for the detailed program of the department. Teachers and other workers usually have their own specific areas of work, but the superintendent bears the responsibility of integrating all their activities into a full rounded program. If joint program planning and evaluation are to become a regular part of their work, the superintendent is to be the one most largely responsible for bringing it about. If thorough effort is made for improvement in the work of the department, he can scarcely escape participation in it.

Furthermore the arrangement of the rooms and equipment comes under the supervision of the departmental leader. Activities for the whole department, such as worship and parent-pupil gatherings, rest largely under the direction of the superintendent. While curriculum materials carry teaching suggestions and resources, the alert superintendent will serve as a resource person for all working in the department, and seek to make available in addition a variety of helpful materials. Frequently such an officer will be elected to membership on the board of Christian education, which participates in decisions on policy and programs; and much helpful information will be gained. The program, problems, and progress of the department may be interpreted to those working in the total program.

It will readily be seen that the departmental superintendent is a key person in bringing about improvement. It naturally follows that such a leader should be given every opportunity to secure whatever training is possible. The church may well invest heavily in such a person. Part of the training will consist in providing such a leader with the various teaching materials called for. Appropriate helps for the age group involved will be extremely useful, such as magazines, books, supplementary lesson aids, and pamphlets, and other items to be found in a first-rate church library. They will, of course, serve not only the superintendent, but through such an officer the staff of the entire department.

The church should make sure that the departmental superintendent has the opportunity to attend training classes and laboratory and demonstration schools. Few training experiences will do more to equip the superintendent to engage intelligently and effectively in the improvement of the work. If there is a professionally trained director at work in the church, or if the minister of the church is well trained and takes an active part in the work of the church school, such a person may give considerable help to the superintendent. It will be seen, therefore, that the departmental superintendent is in a key position and that help and training given such a leader will be a wise investment. Far too many churches fail to realize this fact.

In some churches division superintendents may have supervisory responsibility for an entire division, much as that responsibility has been described here for the department. Such leadership may spread over several age groups. Unless the division superintendent is well trained and can give a generous amount of time to the work, it may tend to be quite superficial; but a capable superintendent may discover major areas of service and identify workers in special need of guidance and render very great assistance. Such a supervisor may concentrate on working with and training department superintendents to function as supervisors for their own groups.

The Helping Teacher. An increasing number of churches are putting into service what may be called a "helping teacher" or a "roving supervisor." This is often the case where there is no trained director or where the school is so large as to require such a worker in addition to other staff members. Since the educational program engages the services of a large number of people with little or no training and experience, it will be most helpful to make available to them a leader with more training and wider experience. Such a person will be available for counseling, observation, and demonstration teaching. Frequently a public-school teacher or administrator will be willing to undertake such a service. The training and experience of such a person may be of great help to those serving in the church school. It is quite likely that such supervisors will need to make special preparation in transferring to religious education.

In many churches the helping teacher will be one selected from among the constituency or from the church-school staff who by reason of training or experience is qualified for such service. In some cases a promising member of the staff will be urged and enabled to take special training that will make such service possible. Attendance upon training classes, participation in a laboratory school, abundant opportunity to observe, and work under some professionally trained person are among the means of training such a person might secure. Wide reading and individual study will help prepare one for guiding workers. It is not wise to conceive of such people serving with no special training, nor on the other hand is it necessary that they have extended training and experience before they can begin to render assistance.

Supervision by the Board of Christian Education. It is entirely possible that much improvement may come about as a direct result of the work of the board of Christian education. It has already been indicated that this board bears the responsibility for the educational policies and program as a whole. It is usually understood that the policies and program will be administered by the executive officers of the board, such as the superintendent, the director, the chairman, and sometimes the minister. If the board takes its work seriously and is willing to devote time and energy to it, it may deal not only with the policies and program as a whole, but also with the program in considerable detail. Committee organization to care for such aspects as the curriculum, personnel, housing and equipment, finances, or program activities on an age-group or functional basis may be a splendid way to bring board members into vital contact with the work. Out of the discussions and committee work vigorous and capable leadership by the board may be exercised. Individuals or committees may be assigned responsibility for following through on suggested plans, dealing with special problems, conducting tests, or securing facts, reporting back to the board. It will probably be best to plan on short-term assignments.

Much will depend on the willingness of board members to take major assignments and spend time in such activities. If some of the members hold positions of leadership in various aspects of the program, such as youth counselor, department superintendent, or other functional or age-group officer, such committee or commission work may take on great significance. In small churches it will often be found most advantageous for the board to hold frequent meetings with the workers' conference or entire staff. Great care will need to be exercised that such a combined group deals with the more important problems and aspects of their work instead of spending time on administrative details or problems of concern to only a few members of the group.

Great emphasis is placed throughout this book upon continuous evaluation of the ongoing program. Members of the board may participate in a great many ways in such evaluation as individuals, as committees, and as a board. From such evaluations should come many suggestions and plans for improvement. The membership should be planned so that members continue on the board for more than one year but on a rotation basis.

The Minister as Guide. Most ministers give some leadership to their church's program of Christian education. Some give it very little leadership, while others make it a major concern of their ministry. There are great traditions for the minister to emulate: the tradition of the great preacher, the pastor, the shepherd of souls, the leader of the congregation in worship. But the tradition of the minister as a great educator and teacher is yet to be established. There are some evidences that it is now in the making. Every minister has an immediate opportunity to share in establishing that tradition, of placing alongside these established traditions that of the conception of the minister as educator.

Many factors will have a part in determining the part the individual minister will play in educational work. Primary among these is his basic attitude toward education, his sense of its importance in the life of the church. If he does not rank it alongside his other ministries, if he does not see in it the great evangelizing force that it is, if he does not regard it as the great "school of Christian living" for young and old, it is quite likely that he will not play a major role in improving the quality of work. If on the other hand he is "educationally minded," is sensitive to the possibilities in Christian nurture, has insight into educational method and understands the scope of the program, and is willing to invest time and thought in the work, he can make a major contribution in this area. In many denominations he is regarded officially as *the* head of the educational program of the local church and ultimately responsible for its success. In other denominations his relation to the educational work may be much more informal. Yet it is difficult to conceive of a minister who will not be vitally interested in the church-school program and eager to do all he can to make it effective.

The Training the Minister Needs. The leadership of the minister will depend also upon his training in the field of Christian education. Men who have been out of seminary for some years, or who never attended, are apt to be quite limited in formal training. Some ministers who lack formal training have made up that deficiency by careful reading and thoughtful participation in the educational program. Most of the recent graduates of theological schools have had the opportunity for some specific training. Many have availed themselves of the more extended training in Christian education afforded today in seminaries and graduate schools. Opportunities for continued study in this field are afforded in special courses in schools of religion, in pastors' schools, in summer leadership and laboratory schools, in local church and community classes, and in the growing volume of literature that is easily and inexpensively available. Certainly the minister who proposes to take seriously the task of supervisory leadership will need to seek specific training for this important and exacting work. Part of this he may take on his own; much of this training he can secure as he works and studies along with workers in Christian education in his church.

Another consideration in this connection is the factor of the time at his disposal, or rather the distribution of time that he makes among the various and multitudinous duties that are his. Many ministers feel that they are too preoccupied with other duties to give but a small fraction of their time to the educational program. One extended study of the minister and religious education showed that of several hundred of what might be termed typical ministers on the average they spent less than 5 per cent of their time on the educational work of the church. One hundred and fifty-three urban ministers who kept careful track of their time for a typical week averaged just over 3 per cent of their working hours at educational tasks. If the minister plans to undertake leadership in Christian education, he will need, first, to plan his time schedule to permit extended contacts with and participation in the educational work. Second, he will need to realize that the better trained he is and the more skilled he becomes, the more he can accomplish in the time he does devote to Christian education. It is not wholly a matter of the amount of time devoted to church-school work. It is a question of whether or not the minister knows how to give skillful leadership in ways that conserve time. The minister who knows *how* to counsel teachers helpfully will engage in these educational activities and still have time for the many other responsibilities of his position. It is largely a matter of the *know-how*. A minister will achieve that by both preparation and participation.

Ways the Minister May Give Guidance. The major contacts the minister has will immediately suggest some of the ways in which his influence and leadership may be felt. He has close contact with all official groups, and his voice will be quite influential in forming attitudes, in providing information, and in determining official policies affecting the educational program. More information is needed in these circles than is generally realized. Too often such discussion is confined to the board of Christian education or workers' conference. When action is desired by the governing bodies of the church, they are often lacking in the information and understanding upon which to act wisely or enthusiastically. The minister should give very careful thought to the matters of primary importance in educational work that should be brought to such overhead bodies, either for information or for action. He might well develop a plan of interpretation to keep working upon throughout the year, selecting matters of primary concern, as the program is outlined and carried through, which should be explained to the church constituency.

One of the most strategic opportunities confronting the minister is his work with the board of Christian education. In a church well organized for education this body should have a most influential part in determining policies, outlining the program, and providing the conditions that will make it possible to carry out the program. The concerned and well-informed minister may serve as a most valuable resource person with the board. Its members could profit greatly from such education. The resources the minister may share with the board are those arising not only from his own knowledge and experience, but also from the rich variety of informing material now available with reference to Christian education, such as books, magazines, pamphlets, curriculums, and program guides. The minister should constantly be alert to bring reports, observations, problems, program suggestions to the board out of his wide and varied contacts. He should, of course, be present at all meetings. Sometimes he may serve as chairman of the board or as discussion leader for some of the sessions. Faithful attendance at the meetings and full participation in all the board's activities will constitute splendid training for the minister.

His work with the workers' conference or general teachers' and officers' council will be varied. Here again he will bring resources of various kinds before the group. He will help interpret aspects of his denomination's program and special emphases. Members of such a group will naturally look to him for inspirational guidance. He should be able to help keep before the entire staff the essentially spiritual nature of their task. He may set himself to a systematic effort to interpret various aspects of Christian nurture, the great beliefs of the church, an understanding of the Bible and its message for today, psychological aspects of religious development, the scope and nature of the church's program, and the missionary outreach of the Protestant church. Many of these possibilities are presented in Chapter IV. Or again he may be helpful in discussing many problems as they are reported out of the ongoing activities by various workers. The workers' conference is one of the most frequently and regularly recurring meetings of the teachers, officers, and leaders. The minister should utilize every opportunity to secure the growth and development of the workers and share with them in their efforts to improve the program.

Some ministers are led into supervisory leadership through their own criticism of the program. A minister of a medium-sized church felt highly critical of the seeming limited use of the Bible in teaching, especially in the lower grades. In preparing himself for a discussion of this problem with the board of Christian education and staff he studied carefully the graded courses of two of the elementary departments. He received along with the course materials the guides for the departmental superintendents. There he read the statement of objectives, the theory upon which the materials and activities were selected, and a very helpful discussion of the possibilities and limitations of the uses of biblical material with children. For the first time in his experience he encountered a careful interpretation of the use of the Bible with young children. As he read, he was won to the point of view of the curriculum writers. He came to see how, in ways he had not known, the Bible was being used. Instead of coming before his staff with criticisms he came with an enthusiastic interpretation of the correct uses of biblical and other materials. A critical attitude was transformed into creative guidance.

The extent to which the minister will share in the more frequent and important meetings of age-group workers' conferences will depend upon a number of factors. These are significant groups, for they plan the program in detail and come together frequently to evaluate its effectiveness. The minister certainly will learn much and may be in a position to make genuine contributions to the program in this way. In all likelihood he will attend more frequently and feel more able in the groups who deal with youth and adult work.

In various other ways the minister may provide educational leadership. Through the pulpit, bulletin, and church papers he may seek to interpret the objectives and scope of the program to the larger constituency. In his calling, especially in the homes where there are children and youth, he may well be the personal representative of all the church has to offer to its members. He will be one of the main channels through which information about the church at large, the movements of his own denomination, and groups within the community may come. These are all important activities and relationships the concerned and alert minister may give himself to generously.

The minister will inevitably find himself entering into some form of personal counseling with members of the staff. He *is* the pastor of the people; he *is* the spiritual guide; he *is* the major interpreter of religion. Individual workers will be in need of various kinds of help, and the minister should stand ready to give it. The extent to which he will be willing and able to give guidance of a more technically educational nature will depend upon his willingness to devote time to it and his ability to be of help to workers in their problems of leadership. Certainly a large field of service lies open to any minister who is capable and willing to give it.

The Director as Supervisor. Undoubtedly the professionally trained director of Christian education is one who normally should serve as supervisor. Such a person is probably better trained in Christian education than anyone else in the church. He is usually paid to devote full time to the program. Unfortunately only a small percentage of the churches across the country are financially able to engage the services of directors. Well-qualified directors are not as numerous as they should be. Where such a person is engaged, a thoroughgoing program of improvement should be possible. In fact, the movement to train and employ such directors represents a marked development of the church's educational vision and concern. The director of Christian education is "something new under the sun." Many churches are still uncertain about the duties of such a worker, and directors find it necessary to clarify their status and function.

It is highly important that the director think of his work in terms of supervisory leadership. His responsibilities spread over such a wide range of activities and so much purely administrative work is assigned to him that actual supervision may easily become a secondary matter. Both the director and the board under which he works must sense the importance of those activities that lead directly to the improvement of the quality of the work. As in the case of the general superintendent all administrative work the director engages in will have its bearing on improvement. Yet too much time and energy may be devoted by the director to administrative and secretarial work to the neglect of those activities that affect more directly the quality of the program. If the director is to become anything more than an administrator or an "errand boy" for every organization, he must intelligently and consciously direct his efforts toward the more definitely educational aspects of his job.

The ways in which the director will serve as supervisor will largely follow the lines suggested in the discussion of the minister. The director will, of course, devote his whole time to his particular task and will thus be able to go into all phases of improvement much more thoroughly. That is the great advantage of having this officer in the church. Usually there has been no one with the training necessary and the time available to go into matters thoroughly in the interests of more effective work. This possibility the director brings into the local church. It is highly important that there be a clear understanding, as the director is employed, as to his major duties. Such an understanding will ordinarily be worked out by the board of Christian education, the director and the minister, subject of course to the confirmation of the proper official body of the church. It is in such an agreement that the possibilities for supervisory leadership will be stressed and some limitation placed upon what may be expected of the director in various aspects of his work. Much depends upon the director's training and his own awareness of essential values in the educational program and his ability to put first things first.

In practically all phases of improvement the director will function most actively. He will lead in discussing basic issues, in policy making, in program planning, in group meetings, in parent co-operation, in holding personal conferences, in working with boards and committees, in counseling pupils, and in evaluation and testing. He will provide initiative, resourcefulness, skill, and continuous follow-up. Employed full time he will be in a position to give time and use abilities growing out of special training. Through assisting workers in every conceivable manner and guiding the program in innumerable ways he should do much to bring about improvement.

Use of Area Supervisory Leadership. One of the means by which various denominations and groups of churches are making available to their constituencies the help of trained educational leaders is through the conference, state, district, and community director of Christian education. Such an officer cannot reasonably be expected to spend a great deal of time with a particular church. Yet his chief responsibility is that of promoting the work of Christian education among the churches of his area. In efforts to bring about improvement in a given local church such a person may make the initial steps toward more intensive supervision. Many churches have secured the services of such a person to make a study of the local situation or to guide the local workers in such a study. Frequently before his visit the church is requested by such a leader to fill out forms that provide for his study and evaluation a full body of facts regarding the present program. The effort to secure and state accurately the facts deemed important by a field worker is in itself the beginning of an improvement process. After careful study of the facts the field director will visit the local church and observe especially the activities of the Sunday school. Frequently he will interview various workers. Then upon the basis of the facts, his observations, and the interviews he will meet with the total body of workers or some comparable group and interpret his findings and make recommendations. These will often be in the form of suggestions for further study and evaluation on the part of the local workers themselves.

The advantages of this kind of procedure will include the observation and evaluation of one not identified with the local situation. He comes to it fresh; his judgment is not biased by local conditions or long-established traditions; he brings wide observation and experience to bear upon the local program, and his recommendations can be made with more freedom and objectivity than might be the case with one closely identified with the program. Also, new interest, enthusiasm, and inspiration may be released by having an "outsider" come into the situation. It lifts workers out of ruts into which they so easily come to work. If such a person is to be used, adequate preparation must be made. Experience uniformly testifies to the advisability of his securing in advance of the visit a full body of information. This would serve to quicken an appreciation on the part of the local church of the conditions and point out factors that are regarded as significant in getting an adequate appraisal of the program. A local church should plan for as many visits with such a person as is deemed necessary or is possible.

Training for Supervisory Leadership. Broad and inclusive training is necessary on the part of one who is seriously to undertake supervisory leadership. The understandings and skills involved in evaluating and improving the program of Christian education are most exacting. Few activities will serve to keep the leader alert and growing as will the responsibility of helping other workers to understand more fully and develop greater skill in Christian education. In the case of the professionally trained supervisor the curriculum of any professional school of Christian education or seminary will indicate the courses generally required of those who are to become directors of Christian education. Experience clearly indicates that beside basic courses in such fields as Bible, theology, philosophy of religion, sociology, and church history special emphasis in training should be placed upon psychology, the learning process, personality development, methods of teaching and group guidance, organization and administration, curriculum construction, counseling, and the procedures of supervisory leadership. Such a list of courses suggests quite thorough training. This is what is recommended by the accrediting agencies in the field of religious education. Those who plan to become directors, ministers of education, or youth counselors in the church are encouraged to earn a master's degree. This involves in many institutions a two-year program of graduate training. With the emergency created by the large number of churches desiring full-time educational leadership and the limited number of qualified persons many churches are engaging persons who have little or no specialized training. Undoubtedly as the church comes to a fuller realization of the kind of leadership that is necessary, more directors will come to their work with graduate training and degrees. An increasing number of ministers in training are seeking to equip themselves with the training and experience necessary to give effective leadership in the educational work of the church. This is one of the most helpful signs of today.

Training the Volunteer Supervisor. The training of the volunteer supervisor will be a matter of providing such a leader with opportunities for preparation. The list of the Second Series Courses in the Standard Leadership Curriculum is suggestive of the wide range of fields that might be covered. These courses parallel those suggested above for the professional workers, but on a much more limited scale. General courses offering a broad foundation of understanding will certainly be a part of the training of such a worker. In addition specialized courses will need to be taken. In training the supervisor to deal with the entire educational program courses covering a wide range of specialized activities are called for. In case such leadership is confined to one age group or function, training should be thorough in that particular field. The church should provide a wide range of training opportunities and surround its workers with every inducement and aid to continue preparation. These will include training classes in the local church and community, experience in laboratory schools, in addition to wide reading and development through continuous service in the program. In the development of departmental supervisors the minister, director of education, and perhaps members of the board of Christian education may be of great assistance. Any minister who is trained and who takes his responsibility seriously faces real opportunities to train supervisors in his own program. He may not himself provide all the training necessary, but he will seek to expose the supervisor in training to some of the opportunities suggested above. What we are pointing out here is *the imperative necessity of each local church's taking seriously the matter of developing one or more persons who are qualified to undertake improvement measurements in the program,* especially if a full-time professionally trained director of education cannot be employed.

For Further Study

1. What leaders, if any, are at prsent assuming definite supervisory responsibility in your church?
2. In studying possible supervisory personnel in your church in the light of this chapter what person or persons offer the most promising possibilities?
3. How should your church proceed in (1) selecting and (2) training the most suitable persons for supervisory leadership?
4. If you are engaged in supervisory work, how may you further equip yourself for such work?
5. How may the officials of the church, the workers, and the total constituency best be prepared for such supervisory assistance?

CHAPTER THREE

Conditions Essential to Effective Education

THE GOAL of the church's educational program is effective Christian nurture. The concern of this text is how we can make that process more successful in achieving the finest and most lasting results. Christian nurture consists of a great many specific elements. Educational method has been defined as the creation and maintenance of the conditions that promote individual and group growth. All teaching-learning situations involve a great variety of conditions. The improvement of religious education is therefore in part a matter of discerning those conditions that are most productive of the results desired. Little improvement can take place without analyzing in detail those conditions, breaking them down into the elements that make up the teaching-learning procedure. Those attempting to increase the effectiveness of teaching will need to know these conditions in great detail and be able to detect those that facilitate and those that hinder the growth of persons and the development of group experience. Fortunately almost anyone can acquire these insights and skills through study, observation, and practice.

The Need for Insights and Standards. It is highly important that this approach to improvement be undertaken in the church for the reason that so many of the conditions under which effective Christian nurture can occur are either violated or only partially fulfilled. Standards of educational work in the church have been uniformly low, and tradition has favored little change.

Parents, pupils, and workers alike have become so accustomed to the many unfavorable conditions that they are accepted and continued without much question. In a certain church some of the workers were attempting to convince the trustees of the necessity for better housing and equipment. In the primary department, for instance, classes were huddled closely together in one room. It was almost impossible for the superintendent to move about. The classwork was conducted in the midst of noise and confusion. The teacher and the superintendent pleaded for separate classrooms, a more appropriate and adequate assembly, and for equipment essential to good work. But some of the trustees and parents, and even the minister, protested the cost and insisted that primary children had always met in such rooms and under such conditions. They were supporting what "always had been" rather than considering the requirements for effective Christian education. Often severe criticism has been voiced over the results of the church's educational program without any attempt to discover just *why* the outcomes are so disappointing. It is the purpose of this chapter to lift up for consideration some of the various conditions that are essential for good education with a view to aiding those who are seeking improvement in analysis, evaluation, and constructive measures. The discussion will begin with the most elementary and objective factors and move into a study of the more intangible and difficult conditions.

The Physical Setting for Christian Nurture. Physical conditions have a marked influence upon the effectiveness of the program. The factors of space, segregation, equipment, light, ventilation, cleanliness, accessibility, and convenience are among those to be considered. The public schools have long since worked out standards and minimum requirements in all these matters. They are met in a general way in most public-school systems. For instance, the standard space per child is sixteen square feet. The light requirement calls for the proportion of one-fourth clear-glass space to the floor space, and the direction of the source of light is taken into account in placing the tables, desks, or chairs. Seats of appropriate height are required for children of different ages, and for the convenience of the various activities in the program movable seats and desks are recommended.

Many careful studies of Protestant church-school buildings have revealed how utterly inadequate most of them are for good educational work. It is true that there has been marked improvement in housing in recent years. One of the encouraging "signs of the times" is the number of churches, small and large, that have built new educational plants or extensively remodeled their old ones to bring them into harmony with the best educational standards. One will find church-school buildings that compare favorably with the best in public education. But the fact remains that the vast majority of church plants are seriously handicapping the work of Christian education. One of the most common difficulties is that of a large room with a number of classes in session at the same time. This condition has prevailed so long and so universally that it is virtually considered standard for Christian education. Many churches in remodeling or building anew follow this grouping of rooms when with foresight and educational understanding they could provide ideal housing conditions without much additional expense. The provision of segregated classrooms is not a luxury but a necessity for good work. One will search in vain for the public or private school of any standing that has two or three classes reciting in the same room at the same time. Public-school teachers and administrators consider it simply impossible to do good work under such conditions. Where complete segregation of the group is difficult or impossible, the supervisor should attempt to reduce the noise and distraction that ordinarily occur when several groups meet in the same room. Various ways have been developed to do this, such as the use of screens (that may serve also as blackboards and bulletin boards), curtains, seating of the members of the group so as to remove distractions, and the use of sound-absorbing surfaces on ceilings and walls. The supervisor should make sure that the necessary effort is made and the small cost met in order that the working situation be improved.

Proper Equipment Is Essential. Such simple matters as the provision of the minimum essentials in equipment affect the success of the program. Few people, parents included, realize how a clean rug facilitates the work of a nursery or kindergarten department, or how helpful it is to have available a bulletin board and a blackboard at eye level for various age groups. Young people are often expected to do serious work in a church-school class without adequate desk or table space for the use of textbook, Bible, notebook, and other essential working equipment. Such equipment is standard and universal in public schools. If pupils, young or old, are so placed that they face constant distractions, are unable to see or hear well, or are uncomfortable in posture or affected unfavorably by atmospheric conditions, their response will be limited accordingly. Some observers have been amazed at the unfavorable conditions found in many churches. What is even more distressing is the fact that many workers seem unaware of the handicaps under which they are serving, and key leaders make no effort at improvement. "Things have always been done that way!"

It is not unusual to find church buildings that are very unattractive and discolored in appearance both inside and outside. All many churches need in order to be greatly improved in appearance is inexpensive and tasty decorations. It is a discredit to religion that the rooms in churches should often be among the most unattractive in the community. Neither is there any excuse for churches to be poorly cleaned, odorous, and unventilated.

The church is the house of God, and unattractive, unkept, and foul-smelling rooms are not only educationally undesirable, but also a discredit to religion. The church building should compare favorably in attractiveness and convenience with the public-school buildings and the average homes of the community. Efforts to improve the teaching conditions may be undertaken in a number of ways. Leaders in each department may study carefully the physical setting for their work to see where improvement is needed. Or a committee of the board of Christian education or the board of trustees may be assigned the responsibility of studying the church plant and of assigning space to the different classes and groups, supervising its upkeep and decoration, providing necessary equipment, and taking care of repairs. A minister, director, or supervisor who develops an appreciation of desirable requirements for good educational work must be constantly on the alert to make suggestions. In all these considerations money is of course a matter of primary importance. Yet extended observation indicates that what is needed even above financial resources is educational insight, conviction, and action on the part of those working in the situation to see and carry through needed improvements. Help in all these matters is readily available from denominational offices and from the bureau of church architecture associated with the National Council of the Churches of Christ.[1] Scores of church architects throughout the country are acquainted with these standards in church-school building. In building or remodeling the educational plant it will be well to make sure that such an architect is employed.

Are Present Groupings Effective? Some plan of gradation and grouping is necessary for the various activities and the different ages in the church. The question is: How effective are the pres-

[1] The Interdenominational Bureau of Architecture, 297 Fourth Avenue, New York 10, New York.

ent groups for the purposes set up and the activities engaged in? What changes are needed? The standard gradation by departments and classes of the church school is commonly known. But the problem of grouping goes much beyond that of the church-school session. Such standard gradation is modified frequently because of local conditions and also because varying groupings are proving more desirable. For instance, in the adult field "young adults" and the "older people" are groups that have come into prominence in church work recently. While close gradation of children and youth has prevailed for certain activities, there is increasing concern for preserving more of the family unity in church life and for bringing the entire constituency into total church fellowship. On the one hand churches with large enrollments and adequate space often keep a single grade as a working unit rather than maintain the three-grade departmental organization. Where it seems advisable, there is a disposition to group two instead of three grades together. On the other hand because of small numbers and limitations of space and leadership many churches find it necessary to combine grades. Here the question is what grades to combine and for what activities. The traditional three-grade departmental group is largely for administrative convenience and does not necessarily represent the best grouping for many of the activities of a well-rounded program. It will be wise in many churches to study the groupings carefully and continuously, and at times to engage in experimentation.

The size of groups is highly important in making decisions. It has been common practice in church schools to keep classes small in enrollment. This may or may not be educationally advisable. Small classes have prevailed for several reasons. They were necessary where several classes met in the same room at the same time. They had to be small for anyone to be heard and understood. The small class meant that the teacher might sustain a much more intimate contact with individual pupils. It provided better opportunity for weektime follow-up and acquaintanceship with the parents. The close personal contact with the pupil by teacher or counselor is highly desirable. No arrangement of groupings should lessen the possibility of such relationships. But with the growing insistence upon a completely segregated room for each class or other group it becomes easily possible for one leader to handle a much larger group. Frequently one will find an entire grade meeting in a class under a head teacher with one or more assistants. Classes with twenty or twenty-five pupils under such conditions are not uncommon. Much depends upon the age under consideration. Fewer classes reduce the number of qualified teachers required. Larger classes are of course highly impractical unless the meeting place is segregated and provided with suitable equipment. Assistant teachers make possible close supervision of individual pupils when necessary. They may give guidance to smaller groups for certain types of activity. They also serve as follow-up and contact persons with the homes. No uniform plan can be recommended. The factors mentioned above should be carefully considered by the local church in planning for the grouping of pupils.

Furthermore there is growing appreciation of the necessity for providing each individual within the church at least one small group where intimate fellowship may be found, where one may have a "sense of belonging." It may be a class, a club, a society, a fellowship cell, or some other functioning unit. The cultivation of genuine Christian fellowship within these various groups is a matter of great importance. The possibility of such an association will be one of the primary conditions to be sought in forming groups and in identifying individuals with them. The fostering of total church fellowship is increasingly becoming a primary concern. One of the choicest values the church has to offer to those who become identified with it is a form of fellowship that is experienced through a wide range of activities, such as study, worship, service, and recreation. One of the most effective ways of bringing an individual from a casual and marginal relationship to the group or the church into a warm vital fellowship is through experiences in such a range of activities.

Maintaining Standards of Attendance. One of the serious hindrances to effective work in the church school is the frequent absence or tardiness of pupils. Pupils who maintain above 90 per cent regularity and 97 per cent punctuality in attendance in the public schools fall far below those averages in the church school. An accurate record kept over a period of time in most churches will reveal a more serious situation than is commonly known. These factors interfer with good educational work far more than most people realize. It is difficult to maintain interest and secure progress if pupils are irregular in attendance. Tardiness interferes with every activity in the program, especially with worship services if they come first in the session. Yet church workers have become so accustomed to these conditions that they often accept them as inevitable and usually make little effort at improvement. That a more satisfactory performance is possible is proved in those churches where an intelligent and consistent effort has been made to secure attendance comparable to that of the public schools. It is entirely possible that there are factors that make it more difficult to maintain high percentages of attendance and punctuality in the church. But most public-school officials know that if they do not insist on high standards and use strict measures of enforcement and skillful motivation, unsatisfactory responses from pupils and parents alike will result. The question of how to secure the desired results arises. Shall punishment, awards, recognitions, of one kind or another be employed? Public-school leaders usually maintain that it is largely a question of getting pupils themselves to accept high requirements and helping them gain satisfaction in meeting them.

Surely the same will be true of the church. The matter of attendance and punctuality is one that should be considered as a church-wide problem. For it affects the church services of worship, attendance at committee and board meetings, and practically every form of church activity. Time is wasted, people are irritated, and ineffective work frequently results because persons necessary for the proper performance of given groups are absent or late in arrival. Tardiness at church services of worship is notoriously bad. Concerted effort throughout the church will usually bring surprisingly gratifying results. But it will require careful planning, consistent follow-up, and accurate record keeping. It is well to stimulate individuals and groups to compete with standards set up and with their own performance rather than with one another or to give prizes and rewards. It would seem perfectly reasonable to recognize in some appropriate manner records of achievement made by individuals and groups.

Significant Information About Individuals. There are of course data regarding individuals of greater importance than records of attendance and punctuality. Such information as the address, relation of the pupil and his parents to the church, grade in school, and assignment to class and department is highly important and should be kept in the church or church-school office. It should be kept accurate and current. Some studies have revealed gross carelessness and inefficiency in the handling of these significant facts. There can be little excuse for churches not having immediately available for any useful purpose carefully kept and informing records. Furthermore such information, kept on a permanent record card, serves as a history of the religious growth of the pupil. Sample forms of such records may be readily secured from denominational headquarters.

There is growing appreciation of other kinds of information that should be secured by those who are working closely with the pupil as teacher or counselor. Information about home conditions, birthdays, hobbies, special interests and talents, neighborhood environment, personality problems, social adjustment, and special needs are exceedingly important and will not ordinarily be made a matter of written record except for the personal use of teacher or counselor. It will be in the nature of working information for the leader dealing intimately with the individual pupil. It will be almost indispensable for the leader to have a notebook with separate pages for each pupil where these items of information can be recorded. Such data may prove invaluable in working with pupils. Securing such information will involve the leader in many contacts with the parents, in conversation with the pupil's public-school teacher, and in planned opportunities for leadership and the assumption of responsibility on the part of the pupil. Such information will become the basis for the more extended counseling program many churches are attempting today. Such counseling will usually be done by the minister or someone specially trained. Surely any worker who is seriously attempting to aid in the religious development of an individual pupil needs all the pertinent data that can be secured.

Limitation of Time. The severe limitations of time under which the program operates is universally recognized. Not only is a once-a-week schedule for classwork inadequate, but the period of twenty to thirty minutes common to most classes is utterly inadequate for the kind of education we desire. This limited period is further curtailed in effectiveness by lateness in beginning and by frequent tardiness on the part of teacher, worship leader, counselor, and the pupils themselves. In many situations there are interruptions to serious classwork due to secretarial and administrative activities. To the extent that the physical setting is unfavorable, to that degree is the effectiveness of the time that is available further curtailed. Frequently these conditions in their totality constitute an exceedingly limited opportunity for nurture and are frustrating to leaders.

All of these factors must be carefully reviewed to locate elements of weakness so that intelligent efforts can be made to strengthen the program. Among the suggestions to be carefully considered are these: (1) The utilization of the full time allotted to the church-school class or other session. If sixty minutes is scheduled, the full sixty minutes should be safeguarded. This means systematic observance of the schedule, arrival of leaders sufficiently ahead of time to do advance checking on working conditions and to greet pupils, cultivation of punctuality on the part of the members of the class or group. (2) An increase in the time set aside for many activities. Few people realize what an additional fifteen minutes would mean to a Sunday-morning church-school session. A seventy-five-minute church-school session is not at all out of the question in a multitude of situations. (3) Extended sessions for certain of the groups in the church school on Sunday morning, making available at least a two-hour period for the program. Recommendations from denominational headquarters include many valuable suggestions of ways to extend and use the time available on Sunday morning. These should be considered carefully by local church groups. With certain groups the Sunday-evening session is being lengthened to include a wider range of activities and a consequent enhancement of the program. The additional time and activities should be integrated into the total program. It is highly advisable for a single planning committee to be responsible for all the sessions and activities entering into the program of any given age group. Weekday sessions for various purposes are becoming increasingly common. For church-school classes these sessions mean added fellowship and recreation, time to work on assigned projects and service activities, and more extended contact between the leader and members of the group. With some groups in the church the weekly meeting may be the primary session. This would apply to the women's society, the men's club, the young adult fellowship, the parents' group, as well as to committees, boards, and councils.

Making Resource Materials Available. As the program has been enlarged and the curriculum enriched, an extended body of helpful resource and supplementary teaching material has been developed. Those who deal with such phases of the program as worship, fellowship and recreation, stewardship, missions and counseling, as well as classroom instruction, will find rich and varied suggestions and materials for making these activities effective. The newer curriculums often include a pupil's text, a pupil's activity book, a teacher's manual or guide, and a parents' magazine or manual. Sets of pictures, both small and class size, are provided with many courses. To some teachers, especially the untrained, these materials appear difficult to use largely because they are so ample. Such courses, while designed to be relatively simple, are prepared on the assumption that those who teach them will give considerable time and study to their proper use. It will be the responsibility of the supervisor to interpret these rich resources to the individual workers and to assist them in using them wisely. Such an array of material is provided, not with the expectation that all of it will be used, either in a given session or throughout the course or series of meetings, but to insure that the alert worker or committee will have an abundance of suggestive resources at hand. A number of conferences with a teacher unaccustomed to the newer courses may be necessary on the part of the supervisor in order to insure effective use and a satisfactory experience with teaching materials.

The variety and amount of such material will suggest that in order for its proper use the supervisor in addition to interpreting it to the different workers will need to make sure that all of these resources are adequately cared for. The modern church is finding it increasingly necessary to provide library space, to classify and file lesson books, magazines, pictures, pamphlets, activity material, audio-visual aids, in order that they may be known and made readily available to all workers. Few things will do more to guarantee alert, growing, and enthusiastic workers than the encouragement and assistance which a well-classified and readily accessible body of resource material will provide. Some or all of these materials may be cared for in departmental or class libraries, where they may be more easily kept and more readily available to the workers. The wise supervisor will seek to discover those persons in the church who have a natural interest and ability in library work who may take over the handling of these resources.

New Help in Audio-Visuals. "Something new under the sun" has appeared in educational circles within the last quarter century, namely, audio-visual instruments and resources. They have transformed the entertainment field and are used extensively in industry, business, and mass communication. The military forces employed them widely during World War II. The public schools are greatly increasing their use of such aids in all phases of their program. New materials and improved instruments are constantly being made available. Audio-visual media have been used in the church from the earliest times until the present. Symbols, architecture, flat pictures, objects, blackboards, exhibits, and bulletin boards have been employed in various aspects of the church's work. The simpler forms and resources are being used increasingly with the clearer understanding of their effectiveness and with the availability of an enlarging body of resource material. The newer instruments and resources are commanding serious attention, and wide experimentation is now taking place. The slide and filmstrip projector, the sound motion-picture machine, the playback and the tape recorder are among the media that increase the effectiveness of many aspects of Christian education. Radio and television are forms of education and communication that may be used by the church, the full impact of which no one seems able as yet to predict. Much depends upon the vision, alertness, resourcefulness, and concern of religious leaders.

The present extent of the use of audio-visuals by the church may be indicated by data from a study of one of the major denominations. Briefly summarized the findings are as follows: 76 per cent of the local churches were found to be using one or more of the newer types of equipment, 61 per cent had access to a motion-picture machine, 52 per cent had available filmstrip and slide projector, and 47 per cent used record players. These media are employed over a wide range of church activities, the most frequent uses being in the following order: entertainment and fellowship, worship, information with other materials, and program fillers. One fact clearly revealed by the study is that there is wide usage without adequate understanding of and preparation for the most effective use of these aids.

Audio-Visuals Improve Teaching. Practically all researches into the effectiveness of audio-visuals clearly indicate that they can improve many teaching procedures. The increase in comprehension of knowledge, retention of information, and mastery of various skills is in many instances from 25 to 50 per cent greater with proper use of these media than without them. The results of such studies leave no doubt as to the significant contribution audio-visuals may make. To supplement the spoken and printed word by visualization in varied forms and to combine audio with visual presentation means that all ages, and particularly children, may be greatly aided in understanding the Bible. We have little idea of the assistance that may thus be given pupils in understanding some of the more familiar Bible teachings when the words, scenes, and persons involved are interpreted visually in the setting of the country, culture, customs, and age in which the teachings originated. A tremendous burden has been placed upon children hitherto in their effort to comprehend the meaning of much of the Bible without any adequate appreciation of the conditions prevailing with reference to events and teachings being studied. To see through motion pictures people living as they actually lived in Palestine at the time of David or of Jesus adds a wealth of appreciation to their study. For youth to get through flat or projected pictures an accurate portrayal of social conditions affecting people whom they are studying but cannot observe firsthand means they will understand far better the situation with which they are dealing. Mission fields with their problems, opportunities, and needs may be brought vividly and helpfully near to people in the local church. Attitudes may be formed much more easily and permanently, ideas established, and strong motives developed through these powerful new media. Verbalizations and abstract ideas that frequently have far less meaning than we realize may be given interpretation and dramatization to make them richly meaningful. The meager firsthand experiences of pupils may be transcended by accurate and forceful presentation of the experience of others. Many highly valuable audio-visual resources for leadership development are being made available. Local workers should be made acquainted with these.

The most urgent needs in this new development undoubtedly are, first, to help workers in local churches understand how much these new resources may contribute to the work of Christian education; second, to acquaint them with the growing body of materials that are now available; third, to train them in the most effective ways of utilizing these instruments and materials. Principles and procedures coming out of their effective use in public-school, industrial, and military situations can now be studied. Religious educators are also developing principles and procedures for their effective use in the church. It is highly important that church workers come early to understand that audio-visuals are not *substitutes for* but *aids* to the programs, teachers, curriculums, and teaching methods already developed. They possess in themselves no unfailing magic. Much misuse is occurring because of failure to study their proper application and adaptation to Christian education. The splendid materials available often are not being employed because leaders in key positions are not acquainted with them or are unskilled in their proper use. Some leader in each church must undertake the task of becoming familiar with this field and of training the entire staff of workers in the effective use of audio-visuals. In most churches the minister or director will give initial leadership. Each church should attempt to discover and train lay people who may assume at least a part of this responsibility. The supervisor will be concerned to make sure that these old and new "conditions" of learning be provided throughout the program.

Co-operation of Parents a Vital Necessity. As a means of making religious education more effective one thing is becoming clear, namely, that the home is still the central agency of religious nurture. While the effectiveness of the home as a place of religious development has varied from century to century, no religion has placed a higher value on home life or assigned to parents a greater responsibility than has the Christian Church. But with the development of the modern program of Christian education in Protestant churches there has been a growing disposition for the church to assume a larger share of responsibility in education with a consequent lessening of concern felt by the parents. Recent years have witnessed a renewed realization that no person or institution can take the place of parents. A major crusade is now being carried forward by denominations, individually and collectively, in parent education and home co-operation.

Several objectives are being sought:

1. To arouse parents to a renewed appreciation of their role and that of the home in the religious education of children

2. To help train them in the full and effective discharge of their responsibility in this area and to acquaint them with and enable them to use the greatly improved resources now available

3. To encourage them to participate in program planning, in sharing in the discussion of problems in Christian nurture, and in evaluating the results being secured both in the church and in the home

4. To enlist them in definite forms of service in church and community as teachers, counselors, club and recreational leaders, and similar kinds of activity

Many ways of working with parents will need to be explored. They should be invited to share in whatever plans are worked out in the local church. Success will be shared in proportion as the effort is centered in the individual child. Few things get the response of a parent as does something that *concerns his child.* Therefore activities and meetings that relate to some aspect of the program immediately involving their children and youth now will constitute the best chance of securing at least the initial co-operation of parents. Among the simple steps that may need to be followed are these:

1. Be sure to provide parents with ample information regarding the program. Ignorance and misunderstanding do not constitute an adequate basis for intelligent co-operation. Do not assume too much. One of the most common reasons for the failure of parents to co-operate with some particular project related to the program of their children is the failure to make clear to them just what is expected on their part. One of the encouraging signs of the times is the enthusiastic response that comes from parents when adequate information is given and specific forms of participation are made clear.

2. Invite parents to share in plans being developed and in the

discussion of problems that arise. Few things will challenge them more than the sense of participation and responsibility. And they should be in at the beginning. They will usually make a real contribution. A supervisor was greatly concerned about some of the members of the high-school fellowship. Their conduct, especially at the evening meetings, worried him greatly. He wrestled with this problem for some time before it occurred to him to call in some of the parents. Their first conference in his home was most fruitful. He discovered that some of them knew at least as much about the problem he had been facing as he did. Others were utterly unaware, but gravely concerned when informed of the situation. Out of their joint consideration came not only suggestions for action, but also definite offers of help. He found it difficult to bring the meeting to a close and found them eager to follow this initial conference with other group meetings.

3. Plan definite things for parents to do, if indeed they do not arise in the planning conferences. Newer curriculums suggest activities for the parents. Some of them provide magazines or parent resources definitely related to the curriculum. Most supervisors can modify or extend these suggestions from experience and knowledge of the immediate situation. Give opportunity for parents to offer ideas.

4. Encourage parents to represent the needs and provisions of children and youth to the church constituency as a whole. Congregational attitudes and support will be needed greatly in any forward-looking program.

5. Place those who are capable in positions of leadership and service in the church. Parents have always made up a major portion of the church-school staff. Parent training and leadership classes should provide a steady increase of parents capable of such service.

6. Encourage them to help in creating a community environment that enhances the chances of their children's growing up

as Christians. They will find many opportunities for concrete types of service in the community that contribute to this end.

It will be the responsibility of the supervisor to work steadily with the various leaders and groups just mentioned to promote this phase of improvement. Among his opportunities will be the following: (1) to secure parent participation in the planning sessions of the various departments and groups; (2) to study the local situation, its needs, peculiarities, and possibilities; (3) to keep thoroughly abreast of developments and to examine continuously the new resources that are being released, bringing them to the attention of people in the local situation; (4) to assist parents and various leaders to carry out the responsibilities accepted by them; (5) to initiate and assist in experiments in this phase of the program; (6) to acquaint workers and parents with the larger opportunities for study and training to be found in denominational and community training conferences and national or regional workshops, and secure representative attendance. One scarcely dares to set limits to what might be done in any given local church when the minister, director, or supervisor gives challenging, resourceful, and creative leadership to those who are willing to think, plan, pray, and work to the end that church and home may unite in intelligent concerted efforts in Christian nurture.

Enlisting the Total Person. One of the significant principles of effective educational work is that of "catching up the total person" in whatever activity is considered essential for learning and development. The application of this principle to Christian education is particularly important because of the fragmentary, infrequent, limited, and superficial contacts that are maintained with so many of those participating. It is a wonder that churches accomplish as much as they do in the light of these limitations. Efforts to improve the effectiveness of Christian education should certainly be concerned with the fuller realization of this principle in church work. It may be stated thus: Growth takes place most significantly in those experiences in which the individual thoroughly commits himself to the immediate world about him. He should share with an intensity of personal interest that through which he is passing. His complete personality should become absorbed. There should be thoroughgoing assent of his total self to that which he does or wants to share.

How can this conception of education be applied more fully in the program of the church? There are a number of ways. Anyone acquainted with camping knows that it is one of the most dynamic forms of character development. Churches are exceedingly wise in their current emphasis upon camping in their program for all ages. Few educational experiences seem to enlist the total person in the full round of activities of which they are a part as camping does. These activities are of such a varied character and are provided under conditions that are so appealing and absorbing in nature that a full response of the person is achieved in a way that rarely occurs in other phases of the program of Christian education. This is also true of the vacation church school. There is opportunity for the pupil to engage in a variety of activities and to get well acquainted with fellow students and adult workers. Its sessions have a frequency, intensity, and continuity that make this kind of school highly effective. It will be understood readily that the longer vacation school is to be preferred. The "parochial" school is, of course, a most effective way of applying this principle to education. But because of other factors involved this type of school does not commend itself to the vast majority of Protestant denominations.

The kind of education we are discussing goes on with real effectiveness in the home that is thoroughly permeated by the Christian spirit, where all activities and relationships are maintained upon a deeply religious basis. The diversity of relationships, the multiplicity of activities, and the complete absorption of persons in the business of living together are aspects of home life and nurture that are hard to excel. The current emphasis among the denominations upon parent training and Christian home life is timely. The all-important thing is that more and more of the educational work of the church may take on this character. There is no simple way of bringing this about. It does mean that when people come to the church for whatever reason, it should be a thoroughly enjoyable and worthy occasion; that experiences take place which move into the deeper reaches of personality; that the number and range of such experiences be increased and enriched; that more of the time, interest, loyalty, and enthusiasm of the individual be "caught up" in the life and work of the church.

In one church concern was felt over the poor response of the junior- and senior-high youth. Some came for the church-school session only. A few came just to the church service of worship. The youth fellowship meeting on Sunday evening was poorly attended and lacking in vitality. Many youth seemed to be quietly slipping out of the fellowship of the church altogether. The council of youth workers, including representatives of the parents and the youth themselves, discussed the situation frankly. It was felt that greater interest and participation on the part of the youth could be secured with the right program and leadership. The outcome of the conference was: (1) a youth choir was formed enrolling the majority of the youth; (2) attractive counselors (husband and wife combinations) were secured for the evening fellowship meetings; (3) the church-school worship was made a training period in worship and hymn singing with the expectation that the young people would attend the preaching-worship services regularly; (4) suitable midweek social and service activities were planned as frequently as the schedule of the young people would permit; (5) all parents were informed of these proposals and their co-operation sought.

The net result of these emphases was that attendance and interest on the part of the youth were felt throughout the total program. Parents, youth counselors, and teachers and the youth themselves were all intelligently and enthusiastically pulling together. There was nothing radically new in the situation, but these program emphases and the participation secured profoundly affected the attitude and response of the youth. The principle under discussion was being more fully practiced and with gratifying results.

Personal relations between the pupil and the teacher or counselor are exceedingly important. The most significant single human factor in the Christian nurture of the young is, as it has always been, the intimate association with capable, contagious, mature religious personalities. Anyone who helps establish these relationships, who extends and enriches them, is contributing vitally to the improvement of Christian education.

For Further Study

1. Certain conditions have been suggested as essential to effective Christian nurture. What other factors do you think are important?
2. Consider your own church's program in the light of these essentials. What conditions are (1) favorable and (2) unfavorable to good educational work? Be specific.
3. Differentiate between the unfavorable conditions in your situation that will yield to immediate modification and those that will require more thorough treatment. How may the latter be incorporated in a long-time supervisory program? In a teacher-training plan?
4. What persons or groups may be assigned definite responsibility for studying and acting with reference to modifying undesirable conditions?

CHAPTER FOUR

Developing Common Understandings

THE NEED *for Group Thinking.* In any effective work in Christian education it is essential that those engaged in the task have a common understanding of what is to be accomplished and how it is to be done. Those who *work* together must *think* together. Many may feel that the development of such a common understanding is not necessary. They may assume that those working in Christian education already have a reasonably good understanding of their work. This is an unwarranted assumption. It has already been pointed out that the great majority of those working in the church school have at best a limited amount of training for their work. Many of the practices common to church school are the outgrowth more of habit and tradition than of careful forethought and planning. Volunteer workers often continue unthinkingly those methods with which they are familiar. "We have always done it that way," is a comment most frequently encountered in church-school work. Many of the ways of doing things have the sanction of the years, but they do not necessarily have the support of the best judgment of those trained and widely experienced in religious education.

With respect to many issues and problems in religious education there is also a diversity of opinion. There are different ways of conceiving objectives. The Christian faith may be interpreted in widely differing forms. There are different theories of the curriculum—also various ways of outlining the program. The best ways of guiding groups in their activities are subject to debate. In these and many other matters workers in the local church may well seek to gain common understandings. Through this process all workers should get new insights and better knowledge of various aspects of Christian education. It may not be possible for all working together to come to common agreement, but it is essential that there be developed a basis upon which the program can be planned and by means of which leaders may proceed even where there is difference of opinion.

Basic Concepts of Christian Education. The supervisor should discuss with those with whom he works the basic concepts of Christian education that are to be made operative. If the supervisor attempts changes or makes evaluations on one basis and those with whom he works operate with quite different ideas, there is apt to be confusion and disagreement throughout. One reason the church secures the services of a director or selects one of its own leaders to guide workers is that such a person has better training and wider experience than his co-workers. The first principle upon which this person acts is to share his understandings of what the program requires for effectiveness and to seek to lay down with the workers the bases upon which they will work together. The one attempting to guide the improvement process is the one most responsible for carrying forward the program of common study.

Often such co-operative study will be carried on by the board of Christian education. In many cases the entire group of workers may be included. If there is no director of religious education, the minister will most likely be the leader, although a capable chairman or other member may render signal service in this connection. The opportunity or necessity for such co-operative study may arise as the group (1) undertakes a careful review and evaluation of their entire program, (2) attempts to rethink objectives, (3) considers the curricula to be used, (4) studies the problems involved in manning the program with capable trained leaders, (5) seeks to enlist the wholehearted co-operation of parents, and (6) prepares for a building or remodeling project. All of these matters call for continuing and systematic study. If such a study includes most or all of the working staff, so much the better.

Some of the most important aspects of the program that require common study will be considered here as a guide to those attempting to bring about improvement. They will be given brief suggestive treatment rather than thorough discussion. The extent to which they will be dealt with in the local group will depend upon the sense of need, the leadership available, the degree of training of the workers, the manner in which the supervisor plans to work, and a number of other factors. Since there is such a large turnover in the working personnel of most churches each year, it will be necessary to share interpretations and engage in common study over and over again. New workers will be entering the service all the time, and they must have adequate opportunity to come to full understanding of their duties and responsibilities.

Thinking Together About Christian Beliefs. There is great need for workers in the local church to study together the theological foundations upon which their work rests. The importance of the theological issues involved in Christian education is easily seen. An understanding of these foundations is essential in any adequate appreciation of the nature and method of religious nurture. In fact, the position one takes on many of them determines in large part how one goes about the work of education. At present vigorous discussion of the theological foundations of Christian education is heard in many quarters. There is by no means unanimous agreement among these qualified to speak. These issues have to do with (1) the nature of God and the way his Spirit operates upon and within personality; (2) the nature of man and how he is saved and becomes religiously mature; (3) the relation of such beliefs to the processes of education; (4) the person and work of Jesus, and the way in which our beliefs here are related to the nature of the individual; (5) the nature of the church and its relation to the individual, to society, and to the kingdom of God; (6) the part men have in realizing or establishing the reign of love and righteousness, and any number of other theological questions.

These theological issues are somewhat involved and difficult to deal with. The question naturally arises: Can average church workers deal with them with satisfaction? They must attempt to. There is no alternative. Local workers must achieve as clear and helpful an understanding as possible of the theological bases upon which their work rests. Denominations are providing a growing amount of helpful literature interpreting these beliefs, and increasing numbers of classes and schools are being held in which workers may get assistance. Workers in any church will use every opportunity to study together in this field. The supervisor in many cases will guide the study. In all likelihood the minister will be the one to carry a major responsibility in directing such activity or serve as a principal resource person.

Workers Seek Help. A junior teacher complained to the director of Christian education at the close of a morning session of her lack of understanding in dealing intelligently with problems in the interpretation of the Bible. As she talked, the director realized that she felt deeply her inadequacy. Others in the same department seemed to have the same feeling. "Would you like to share together a number of study sessions on approaches to the Bible?" asked the director. They were unanimously enthusiastic about it. (The director recalled his vain attempt a few months before to organize a class on this same topic.) Workers in other departments, when they learned of the proposal, expressed a desire to participate. In the end most of the working staff of the church school met for ten one and one-half hour sessions where they attempted under the leadership of the director, assisted at times by the minister, to develop a common approach to and understanding of the Bible. Of course the discussion included constant references to the lessons various teachers were using and to the questions pupils were raising. These people went forward in their work with a knowledge of the Bible that made them more confident and competent. It also enabled the supervisor to work more closely and continuously with them because they had developed common understandings in this area of their joint work.

In another church the teachers confessed great uncertainty regarding some of the major beliefs of the church, the nature of God, the person and work of Jesus, the doctrine of sin and salvation, immortality, and the relation of such beliefs to the work they were doing from Sunday to Sunday. The minister responded enthusiastically to their request for help. For several Sunday evenings they gathered informally in the parsonage and, led by the minister, gave careful thought to their own personal convictions on these theological issues—also how they might interpret them to the pupils of various ages in their groups. They not only gained help in this regard, but the fellowship they enjoyed, the closer relationship they established with their pastor, and the greater confidence they felt in their difficult task of making religion vital to others were among the rich returns from the time and effort invested. Because of this common understanding they were readily able to discuss these matters among themselves and also with their minister as they progressed in their work.

As will be suggested in the chapter on leadership development, there are numerous ways in which understandings in this area may be developed. The suggestion of books and pamphlets to read, organization of training classes either on an elementary or an advanced level, and provision for personal conferences will be among the means employed to achieve these understandings.

Understanding the Christian Nurture Process. Those attempting to give guidance in religious education should have at least an elementary knowledge of the structure of personality and of how one may give guidance in the development of character. Space does not permit a detailed discussion of the growth-learning process at this point. But it is proper to insist that supervisor and workers give serious and continuous study to the nature of personality, the native forces within human nature that determine the manner and rate of growth, the laws of learning, how the teacher may guide the process, and how the resources of the Christian religion are utilized in the learning-maturation process. These are among the most significant questions that concern Christian educators today. They are difficult to deal with adequately. The position one takes with reference to the theological issues just mentioned will have most important implications for the questions raised here. It is little wonder that volunteer workers feel that they are dealing with problems concerning which they have very limited understanding.

It is in this area that the professionally trained leader is most urgently needed. Volunteer workers are desperately in need of the kind of assistance that the trained minister or director of religious education should be able to give. Professionally trained leaders too may sense the difficulty of achieving clear and helpful understandings of the nurture process. But they should be able to guide their co-workers in a co-operative search for fuller knowledge. They should know the best literature and seek to make it available. They should be sufficiently keen observers of the actual work going on in the local church to be able to identify success and failure in realizing some of the more important outcomes. They should study together with their associates the reasons for success and failure. Few of us will achieve mastery in this difficult area. But all of us can through diligent study, careful observation, and intelligent practice clarify our understanding and improve our skill in promoting the religious growth of those in our care. This is one of the major objectives of whatever supervisory leadership is given in the local church.

Clarifying Objectives. The purposes that guide the program as a whole or in part are exceedingly important. Frequently they are none too well defined by those giving leadership. It is easy to assume without basis that teachers and leaders have a clear notion of the goals toward which they are striving. One of the common sources of misunderstanding and criticism with respect to the ongoing activities of the church school is the fact that the program has been developed or the curriculum prepared with broad inclusive objectives in mind and that those working in the program in the local church are guided by quite narrowly conceived and traditional purposes.

The objectives of Christian education have often been thought of solely in narrow, evangelistic terms. "Winning the individual to Christ and to membership in the church" has been one of the most common statements of purpose. This must ever be the central purpose of Christian nurture. Along with this has been concern for knowledge of the Bible and elements of the Christian faith. Such aims are variously stated. These goals must also always remain basic in the nurture of the church. But with the development of educational theory and practice leaders have become concerned with goals that embrace the totality of living. The many elements that make for strong character and well-rounded personality have found a place in the detailed objectives of Christian education. It is not enough to "win the individual to Christ." He must be helped to bring every aspect of his personality and every activity of daily living under the control of a dominant loyalty to Christ as Saviour. This calls for objectives which include the characteristics of personality development and aspects of daily living.

The process of setting up these objectives for the working group in the local church and making every member intelligent concerning them is something that the supervisor should plan carefully. He will need to encourage creative group thinking. He will first need to make the group acquainted with the widely accepted and well-formulated statements of objectives, such as are found in the literature of the National Council of Churches and of the various denominations. He dare not assume that all the workers have these clearly in mind and understand them. They will need to be reviewed and discussed and their application to the local program clearly seen. Their formulation in terms of the different age groups will be found in much of the literature coming into the local church. But nothing can take the place of the local workers' thinking together about their application and stating them in terms of their own understanding and efforts. Leaders coming into contact with pupils of various ages should be encouraged and helped to get the problems, needs, and interests of their pupils as clearly and fully defined as possible; for out of these will grow many of the most significant purposes guiding the program. The process should be a shared one, for there is much stimulation in the exchange of ideas and experiences. Frequently out of such co-operative thinking will come insights and understandings not otherwise attainable. It will be the function of the supervisor to promote such activity.

Setting Up Special Objectives. Workers should be concerned about ultimate, long-term objectives as well as immediate special outcomes. Most of the formulated statements of objectives are concerned with ultimate purposes. In a local church workers may be led to concentrate on one or more of these. But in all likelihood it will be found necessary or advisable to set up special objectives. These may have to do with particular needs that have been uncovered, or problems requiring solutions, or purposes that the church is especially eager to see accomplished. Pupils of a certain age group may be seriously lacking in adequate recreational opportunities and facilities; fellowship within some groups may be poorly expressed; attendance, both in punctuality and regularity, may have fallen very low; evangelism may not be carried forward consistently through the youth departments; parent co-operation needs to be encouraged and directed; or greater emphasis should be placed upon world outlook and social concern in certain of the departments. Any one or all of these items may be incorporated in special objectives that may determine some of the activities, curriculum materials, and other details of the program. Many denominations have developed programs with special objectives and emphases which have been interpreted in the literature going to the local churches. These special emphases will need to be studied by workers in the local church and, if acceptable, incorporated in their own programs.

In a certain church the workers in the junior-high department spent considerable time in the fall retreat in reviewing their program, studying the young people, and setting up the objectives for the coming year. They had before them the full statement of objectives found in the literature of their denomination. Among the outcomes they decided upon were these:

1. To attempt to develop a stronger spirit of fellowship and loyalty. This objective arose from the realization that members of the department came from different neighborhoods and from different public schools which made it difficult to unite them into a functioning fellowship.

2. To seek to identify those youth who seemed "on the edge" and to try to bring them into full participation in the life and

activities of the department. This objective was based upon the knowledge that certain youth participated irregularly in only a few of the activities of the department.

3. To make a more serious follow-up on absentees. It was discovered that frequently no particular effort was made by teacher or officer to discover the cause of absence and to challenge pupils to prompt and regular attendance.

4. To canvass carefully the home background of each of the pupils and to work more effectively with the opportunities represented in their home situations. In dealing with objectives 2 and 3 they discovered factors in home conditions that were very helpful in dealing with individual youth.

5. To multiply the occasions when the young people and their parents would be brought together in fellowship and activity in the church.

6. To ask different parents to share in staff meetings. Such participation would bring into the discussion the viewpoints of parents, would be helpful to parents in their understanding and co-operation, and would equip them to interpret the program to other parents.

7. To make sure that each of the young people who had not previously declared himself a disciple of Christ and had not taken first steps toward church membership was definitely challenged to do so.

Before the group adjourned, they had considered various ways in which each of these special objectives might be accomplished. They went into the winter's work with intelligence and enthusiasm because of these meetings. The superintendent reported these objectives to the workers' conference for their information and to the board of Christian education for their approval and further suggestions.

A Children's Group Reconsiders Objectives. In a kindergarten department the workers were conscious of criticism from some of the parents over the seeming neglect of the use of biblical material in the program. The superintendent called these parents to meet with the teachers to study together the needs and limitations of that age, the program and curriculum proposed by their denomination, and the activities making up their own session and the responses the children were making. The parents were invited to visit several of the sessions to see for themselves how the program was carried forward. Following this the same group attempted to set forth clearly and definitely, not only for themselves, but also for the total group of parents, the outcomes sought through the kindergarten department. It became clear to the parents that specific objectives had been determining the content and activities of the sessions and that these had been set up in the light of denominational objectives and those growing out of intimate knowledge the teachers had of the needs and limitations of children of that age. The parents were able to help the teachers to understand some of the reactions of the pupils, and they were enlisted to assist in the department according to a schedule of rotation in service.

It is exceedingly important that leaders come to have a consciousness of genuinely Christian purposes in their work. It is very easy for them to be content with surface outcomes. Knowledge of the Bible is needed? Yes. But not for its own sake. Such knowledge must be brought into functional relation to problems and needs in the religious development and daily living of the pupils. Understanding of and interest in people of other races are sought? Certainly. But something is needed that goes beyond mere satisfaction of curiosity or the development of a sentimental attitude of friendliness that never expressed itself in really helpful ways either to pupils or to those they seek to befriend. So much activity can and does go on in the church today that fails to fulfill any significant purpose because the objectives are not defined in the beginning or there is failure to state them in terms highly significant to worthy Christian living. This is an area of concern that supervisors should consider with workers time and again.

Nature and Scope of the Program. Workers must understand the nature and scope of the modern program of Christian education. They need to realize that it has been revised and enlarged. It is not to be thought of primarily as a Sunday-morning session an hour long and usually with a limited range of activities. Rather it embraces all the teaching functions of the church, the total range of ministries the church attempts to render to its constituency. Thus it is that the program not only deals with Bible study and worship in the more limited and traditional sense; it also embraces vital fellowship, training in stewardship, concern for the application of the gospel to the problems of the social order, effort to provide pastoral care and counseling for young and old, the development of leadership skills, and a sense of participating in the life and work of the church. These activities represent a greatly broadened understanding of the nurture the church should provide. *A church program of Christian education consists of all the activities, materials, resources, physical facilities, and personnel involved in carrying forward the full range of ministries of the church to its total constituency.* Thus it is that the teacher or counselor who thinks that his work and relationship to the members of his group consist only of a brief period of instruction on Sunday morning or evening needs to be helped to understand that in order to achieve the kind of development the program seeks, the range of activities and the kind of relationships he participates in with the pupils will need to be greatly extended. The process of improvement will certainly include efforts to develop this understanding among all those participating in any church work.

Ways of Working with Groups. There are two types of procedure especially that workers should study together: first, ways of working with groups; and, second, ways of working with individuals. A vast amount of church work is done with and through groups—groups of all kinds. They include classes, clubs, committees, cells, boards, departments, societies, and fellowships. The various insights and skills involved in working with these groups constitute the methodology of education. The understanding and mastery of these methods become the common concern of all those participating in leadership. "Teaching religion" has been commonly thought of as "teaching a class." But the program of Christian education described above calls for all kinds of groupings and employs a wide range of activities. The narrower concept of method is being supplanted by the broader idea of "ways of guiding groups." The idea of "courses of study" is giving way to the concept of "units of guided experience." These newer concepts, methods of leadership, forms of human relationships, organizations of content and experience should be the subject of continuous study on the part of the supervisor and the workers.

Basic points of view represented in each of them need to be discussed and their implications for the ongoing work understood. For instance, one may approach teaching from the authoritarian point of view, that is, believing that the teacher is an authority who "presents" the material to be "learned" by the pupils. He directs the process, makes the assignments, evaluates the program, and otherwise controls the teaching situation. Or teaching may be regarded as a democratic, creative, co-operative enterprise in which pupils, or members of the group, plan, discuss, explore, evaluate, and otherwise carry forward together the "unit of study" or "program of activity" in full co-operation with the teacher or leader. Each of these basic points of view, together with some variations, have important implications for the work of the local church. If one position is taken, then the ways of working with people, the use of content and resource material, the nature of some of the outcomes sought, and the range of activities engaged in will be quite different from those that follow from another point of view.

Curriculum and program suggestions from denominational headquarters need to be explained carefully to those who use them to discover upon what conception of method they have been planned. Such a procedure will tend to create a far better understanding of and attitude toward the program and curriculum materials than is frequently the case. Much of the criticism in the local church of literature coming from "headquarters" would be lessened altogether if workers were helped to a fuller understanding of just why it has been planned as it has. One of the major difficulties or weaknesses of much religious education is that the detailed procedures of the leader with the group have not been guided by any clear understanding of the theories and principles underlying such group activity. Most of the courses are now planned as "units of guided experience." They are flexible, suggesting a variety of activities, providing much more material than can be fully used in single sessions, and enabling the teacher to continue the study for as many sessions as seems best.

Creative Group Activity. In considering ways of working with groups the whole range of group procedures needs to be studied. The more traditional and limited lecture method will strongly appeal to some, especially older workers. Some teachers may be inclined to use the simple question and answer procedure because of inexperience and a feeling of inability to go beyond this form of class activity. But the newer conceptions of method present a variety and wealth of suggestions for making work with groups thoroughly enjoyable and highly effective. Skillfully directed discussion, project activity, creative drama, group dynamics, directed conversation, commission work, group silence, audio-visual methods and resources are all terms suggestive of group-work experiences that are transforming many uninteresting, inactive, unrewarding teaching-learning situations into those that are alive with interest, enthusiasm, participation, and fruitful outcomes. They are developing teachers and leaders into alert, resourceful, adaptable, and skilled workers because of the training provided in the very process of sharing in such group activities, the challenge presented to them to be creative, and the unsuspected abilities that are brought into functioning. These possibilities need to be interpreted to the entire working staff, both by discussion and demonstration. They relate not only to the formal class session on Sunday morning but also to the various evening fellowships, committees, boards, women's societies, and kindred groups. In any situation where people come together to study, to worship, to enjoy fellowship and recreation, to attend to responsibilities connected with the church program in the community and in its wider relations, there group procedures of some kind are inevitably involved. The question is: How effective and fruitful will they be? The supervisor faces a great opportunity to interpret these more creative methods to workers and to guide them in their more effective use.

Ways of Working with Individuals. Another major method of Christian nurture is that of direct person-to-person relations. Probably the most significant thing about the ministry of Jesus was his concern for and work with the individual as such. This has always been true of Christianity at its best, and certainly of Christian education. The traditional emphasis in evangelism has been upon a "win them one by one" process. There is nothing new in this idea. It is true, however, that the modern program of religious education is placing ever stronger emphasis upon work with individuals. With the newer insights of modern psychology and psychiatry, and with the skills being developed in counseling, it is now possible for us to work with more intelligence and effectiveness with persons.

Such insights and skills are those that should be sought and studied by workers in the local church. Such simple matters as proper enrollment procedures and the nature of the information that should be secured about each individual pupil, the form of cumulative record that should be kept, the nature of the most desirable home contact and follow-up, and the ways of developing freedom of relationship and rapport between the pupil and the teacher are exceedingly important. The supervisor and those with whom he works need to explore together the more fundamental aspects of personality development and the ways the leader may facilitate and enrich that development. Unless there is some common understanding and general agreement about these matters, there is apt to be confusion and ineffectiveness in the program. While most workers will need to confine their activities to the more elementary aspects of the study of individuals, there is really no limit to the thoroughness with which any group or individual worker may study in this field. The supervisor may himself become sufficiently well trained to carry a heavy responsibility in counseling, with both pupils and members of the working staff. Many ministers are taking training in this phase of church work and will be able to render increasingly valuable service.

Appreciating the Necessity of Evaluation. There has been little serious effort to evaluate the results of Christian education in the local church. One obvious reason is the difficulty of making evaluations that are reliable. But another reason is that not many workers are disposed to check carefully on the results of their work. They seem to be content to move along from week to week doing the things that keep the work going without serious inquiry into its effectiveness. True, they have a strong desire to bring about religious development. They sincerely hope that the outcomes sought are being achieved. But aside from some superficial evidences of success or failure they have slight knowledge of how well they are doing in their work.

It will be the task of the supervisor to lead the workers into an appreciation of the importance of evaluation in improving the program. In every way possible he will interpret the necessity of more studious concern over the results of teaching and leading. Beside discussions in general meetings, evaluation can be made a most natural aspect of program-planning sessions. It is here that the specific outcomes to be sought will be determined. The activities and materials to be used will be selected. The methods of guiding individuals and groups will be discussed. If the planning is well done, the basis for careful evaluation will be laid. Those who plan and carry out the plans will most naturally be concerned to check upon results achieved. If they are given proper guidance, they frequently will prepare some simple test forms, or questionnaires, or other means of getting at the results. *This phase of improvement is considered so important that a chapter will be devoted to it.* The point being made here is that among the areas in which common understanding among all workers should be developed, the appreciation and possibilities of evaluating outcomes is most important. A concern for a better knowledge of the results being achieved may well begin with the board of Christian education. Through their interest and activity the entire staff of workers may be concerned. One or more workers identified with a department may ultimately affect the attitude of all taking part in the program.

Ways of Developing Common Understandings. Throughout this chapter suggestions have been made regarding *how* common understandings may be achieved. It may be well to summarize these and indicate other means of joint study. Among the opportunities that should be considered are the following: (1) workers' conferences; (2) board of Christian education meetings; (3) departmental staff sessions; (4) leadership training classes and laboratory schools; (5) special meetings with the director or minister; (6) reading of books, magazines, and pamphlets; (7) correspondence courses; (8) individual or group study of lesson materials, especially the teaching helps; and (9) common experiences workers may have together in church worship, listening to sermons, and entering into the fellowship of the Christian community. It will readily be seen what a wide range of opportunities lies at the disposal of any group of church workers to come into a better understanding of the basic principles and methods involved in Christian nurture.

Creating Favorable Conditions. It is highly important that all workers become keenly aware of the many details that condition the success or failure of their work. Educational insight and skill come largely from knowing the factors that are essential to effectiveness in any given relationship and type of activity. Those working in the church school frequently become so accustomed to conditions that seriously limit the success of their work that they are insensitive to them and make little or no effort to bring about better educational situations. Some improvement that is brought about will come as a result of someone's ability to evaluate a teaching-learning situation, to identify conditions that need to be changed, and to seek to bring about desired improvement. It is highly essential that all workers come to understand fully the broad and inclusive interpretation of the church's educational program as it is now presented in the literature of most denominations.[1] This more than anything else will stimulate them to study the provisions and conditions that will improve the quality of Christian nurture in their own church.

[1] For this broader interpretation of the church's educational program see my *Christian Education Through the Church.*

Developing Common Understandings

For Further Study

1. To what extent do you share the central conviction of this chapter that common understandings need to be developed among workers?

2. What additional aspects of Christian education do you think should be treated in the manner suggested in this chapter?

3. Select by yourself or in co-operation with others the areas in which there is the greatest need of common study in *your* church. Indicate how you would proceed to promote such study.

4. How may continuous effort along this line be made in your church? Who should assume major responsibility for such activity? How may such study be incorporated in the teacher-training program?

CHAPTER FIVE

Guidance Through Group Activity

S*IGNIFICANCE of Groups in the Church.* An amazing amount of work in the church is carried forward through groups of one kind or another. Boards, committees, councils, fellowships, classes, clubs, commission, and worshiping groups are among those usually found in the church. If one were to list the number and variety of groups operating through a week or month of normal church life, the results would be both informing and surprising. The real essence of the Christian religion and democracy is expressed through the widespread participation of the people in the work of the church. Through groups people are brought into effective relationship with one another, individual personalities are developed, leaders are given opportunity for the expression of their capabilities, and individual and group responsibilities are discharged that could not occur as effectively and wholesomely in any other way. The group experience stimulates thinking, provides for exchange of ideas, and corrects false notions. Creativity and individual initiative are encouraged. A variety of ideas, plans, and suggestions are developed. Angularity of personality is corrected, training in co-operation is provided, individual members are encouraged and inspired through the group, and fun and fellowship are provided that are not otherwise available. Failure to achieve some of the highest values of Christianity and democracy occurs when a few persons or a few leaders assume most of the responsibility and when members of the group are not challenged to participate fully.

The matter of *how* people are brought together to form and function as groups, *how* they express their common interests and carry on their duties, *how* individuals are related to one another, and *how* people secure the kind of development they need are all important considerations that deserve careful study. Certainly anyone responsible for the improvement of the educational program needs to study the fundamentals of group procedure. Insights and skills may be acquired that will immeasurably facilitate the supervisor's ability to deal with groups. Recent developments in the theory of group activity and fresh insights that psychiatry contributes bring the leader a most helpful body of new resources. The term "group dynamics" currently much in use represents something both old and new—old in that many of its procedures have long been in practice, new in the sense that new insights and skills in work with groups are becoming available.

Creative Work with Groups. While many supervisors may feel untrained and inexperienced in working with groups, there are some simple and fundamental points of view and procedures that should be understood and used as far as possible. In working with almost any kind of group the supervisor is concerned to create a situation where people can work co-operatively, where there is a positive, friendly atmosphere. Perhaps the most essential thing is that they have opportunity to identify themselves with a problem, need, or situation. "A problem gives a collection of people a purpose." While a given situation may be "arranged" by the supervisor, the group should begin where the members are in their thinking and experience. Workers will grow and function as they come into contact with the ideas and experiences of others. Every effort should be made to enable the group to grow in unity, to develop the experimental approach, to learn to work together fruitfully, to engage in free and full discussion, and to acquire a feeling of self-confidence and acceptance. Members of the group must be helped to understand the method of work they are using. They and the supervisor should realize that unless the members of the group have worked together for some time, they may not at the beginning be mature as a group. They will have to acquire experience as a functioning unit in order to achieve the results desired. Such a realization will relieve tension and will lessen impatience over initially slow progress. The less experienced the group is, the slower will their progress be. The leader must learn how to work "within" the group rather than from the outside, how to change his relation from a fixed, predetermined status to one of being genuinely a member of the group. There is nothing more important for the supervisor to realize than that leadership is primarily "a quality of group activity," not just the performance of an individual with responsibility or authority. The group experience becomes creative when workers are given the feeling that they are making worth-while decisions, that their suggestions have value, that they are really counted upon to help achieve the outcomes sought by the group. Such an experience serves to release the creative energies and talents of all members. It develops an air of expectancy. All members have a personal stake in what is to be accomplished. The development of understandings, the acquisition of these skills, the sense of knowing how to work creatively with all kinds of groups, and the satisfactions arising from such results in human association are worthy of a lifetime of effort.

Group Guidance Procedure. The schedule that follows suggests the kind of evaluation that may be made of that form of group procedure sometimes referred to as "co-operative group enterprise," "creative group procedure," or "group dynamics." Emphasis is placed upon the group as a whole assuming a large share of or complete responsibility for guiding their own activity, rather than the customary practice of having responsibility rest upon a previously designated leader. Such procedure may assume various forms, but it is felt that the chart that follows will be suggestive as guidance in an evaluation of the effectiveness of this form of group activity. It may be modified and enlarged as the supervisor may wish.

SCHEDULE OF EVALUATION OF GROUP PROCEDURE

Nature of Group: ________________ *Membership* __________
Leadership: Individual _____ committee _____ predetermined __
elected by the group _________ method of change _________
Objectives: ________________ how developed ______________
modifications as group proceeds ______________________
Methods of Procedure: ______________________________
how determined _________ significant issues, questions _____
________________ spread of participation ______________
responsibility carried by all _________ majority ___________
few __________________ movement of discussion __________
ability to move to decisions ___________ to action __________
skills in handling conflicts, deadlock, indecision ______________
Activities engaged in beside discussion: committee meetings __
_______ creative work _______ investigation _______ visitation
_______ observation _______ research _______ recreation _____
Quality of fellowship: definitely Christian ______________ how engendered and sustained ____________________________
Termination of sessions: ______________ plans for continued work ________________
TOTAL EVALUATION _________________________________

Groups Related to the Educational Program. There are certain groups that are naturally and intimately involved in the work of Christian education and especially in efforts to improve the quality of the program. The board of Christian education, the conference or council of workers, functional commissions, parent organizations, the departmental staff, and committees are among the groups with which the supervisor will deal. It will be necessary for the supervisor to identify the individual members of these groups, to study their possibilities and limitations in functioning, and to provide the kind of guidance that will enable them to make their maximum contribution. There is a natural and practical necessity about many of these groups. The board of Christian education must make decisions about policy and programs. The workers' conference needs information, training, and encouragement in their work. Departmental leaders must develop in detail the programs they are to carry out. And committees must have assignments they are expected to discharge. A natural situation prevails therefore for efforts to strengthen the program through the guidance of these groups. They come to grips personally with the pupils, with the activities they engage in, and are involved in procedures that may lead them constantly to evaluate the effectiveness of their work and to seek better ways of doing it.

Laying a Basis for Group Activity. One of the major responsibilities of the supervisor will be to help those he works with to a better understanding of Christian education, its objectives and the methods and resources of the program. It will be recalled from an earlier chapter how important it is that those working together share common understandings regarding their work, how necessary it is to take seriously the development of these shared insights. One of the first things the supervisor will seek to discover is the degree to which those who compose these groups need to study more carefully the nature of the work in which they are engaged and the best methods of doing it. There is a strong tendency for workers to continue traditional ways of carrying on their work. One frequently hears a minister or director complain that the board of Christian education has a very limited conception of the total program of Christian education or of some phase of it. But the minister, director, or superintendent needs to consider the question: What has been done to help the members of the board to gain a full understanding of the various aspects of the program? Skill in guiding groups will be revealed in the way in which such a leader stimulates discussion, brings resource materials to the attention of the members, and points out the relevance of the things discussed to the program under way.

Or it may be that the workers have a very limited knowledge of the range of activities that are embraced in a well-rounded program. It will be helpful if the leader of the group will review with them literature describing the full program as planned by most denominations as well as suggestions found in approved textbooks, in order to increase his appreciation of the opportunities and responsibilities of working with his fellow leaders and their pupils. Often leaders feel critical of workers for failure to provide for basic activities of the program when the leaders have not made sure that the workers have had ample opportunity to come to understand what should be attempted. Even though denominational literature may carry a full explanation of why the program is outlined the way it is, or why the curriculum is developed along certain lines, it will be necessary for those in charge to lead workers in full discussion of such material, not once, but doubtless several times. The use of blackboards and chart displays will help to make things clear and register more lasting impressions. Some of the more important material may be put in mimeographed form and in notebooks where it may become a more personal and permanent record. There are many pamphlets that are invaluable in interpreting to workers various aspects of the program. They are inexpensive and highly practical.

Defining Objectives and Methods of Work. No aspect of the

modern program of Christian education is developed and released to the field without painstaking consideration of the objectives sought. These aims will be set forth usually with great care in the program material or curriculum sent to the local church. They should be accepted as the purposes of those who use the material, even though they must be modified in view of local conditions and often restated in the language and setting of those who teach and lead. It is only thus that programs prepared in denominational offices can take on meaning and vitality for the workers in the local church. These objectives may well be considered by all groups working in the local church, the board of Christian education, the supervisory leaders, the departmental staff, and parents. In some situations workers may develop the objectives of their program independent of outside aid. This will require intelligent leadership, considerable time, and adequate resources. But such activity may be one of the most vital elements in the training of those participating.

Likewise in the use of curriculums workers will need to consider together the best way of adapting the material to the local situation. A group of teachers of intermediates in a local church complained of their failure to interest the pupils in the course selected for them for the quarter. They confessed that they themselves did not feel intelligent and enthusiastic about the study. The supervisor asked the teachers which method of introducing the course to the pupils suggested in the teacher's manual they had used. They all confessed they had not even read the carefully prepared introduction to the course in the teacher's manual where several different plans of introducing the course to the pupils were treated in detail. They went over with the supervisor the objectives of the course. They reviewed the suggested methods of interesting the pupils in the material, and each teacher selected the suggestions he preferred. They discussed the pupil activities that might be attempted. They selected resources outside the course material that might be used. As a result the teachers made a new approach to their work and with greatly quickened enthusiasm and clearer insight. Gratifying results were obtained. In reviewing of the suggested areas of common study in Chapter IV it will readily be seen that a great deal of training of workers as well as improvement of the program may occur through group study of the program and the various methods of carrying it forward.

Program Planning and Evaluation. A junior-department superintendent was finishing her review of the new curriculum unit their department was to start in the fall as the teachers arrived for their first conference on the program. She had pupil and teacher quarterlies ready as well as other resource material with which she planned to acquaint the teachers. She began the conference by giving an over-all interpretation of the unit of work selected for their classes. She reviewed with them the objectives listed in the manual and encouraged them to add some of their own or state them in their own language. Together they considered the nature of the content in both the pupil's and the teacher's books. They discussed the related activities described in the manuals and selected those they thought would be most interesting to their pupils. Resources the superintendent had secured were considered. Some of the pupils needing special guidance were discussed, and helpful suggestions came out of their rather lengthy conference on several of the "problem cases." Further interpretations of the total program were considered, the worship services, the fellowship periods, some of the service projects that might be carried forward during the year, and the various ways parents might carry the part that was clearly theirs. Included in the group were two fathers and mothers of children in the department. They had been invited to share in the conference as representatives of the total group of parents who were expected to co-operate intelligently and heartily. They were present to give parents' reactions to the proposed program and to gain help in interpreting the work to other parents.

Several weeks later the same group met to evaluate the success of their initial sessions with the pupils. Each teacher was asked to report on evidences of effectiveness, the degree of interest and response on the part of the pupils, the extent of the material covered, the way in which the anticipated activities were engaged in by the pupils, special problems that were encountered, and the suggestions each had for further procedure. Each teacher was intensely interested in the reports of the other workers, and many suggestions were made that some felt might be included in their own work. The department superintendent made comments on her observations and her own contact with the pupils during the opening sessions. She led the group in a discussion of activities outside the class session, asking the reactions of the teachers and parents to the worship services in particular. These evaluations made members of the group more keenly aware of the objectives they were seeking to achieve and of their own part in the total program as it was being carried forward. The parents reported their reactions and discussed ways of relating other parents more closely to the work of the department. The unanimous feeling among the members was that this experience of group planning and evaluation should be held frequently.

Co-operative planning is one of the most natural and effective ways of improving the program and training those participating in it. Those engaged in planning will have a vital concern for their own part in the program. They will usually feel the need for all the help they can get. The leader knows there must be full understanding and enthusiastic co-operation on the part of each member of the staff. Experience reveals how (1) group thinking enriches the ideas of each member, (2) a variety of methods of procedure are suggested, (3) unexpected resources are uncovered, (4) enthusiasm grows as the program takes shape, and (5) additional responsibilities are more readily assumed under the stimulus of group procedure. The skillful leader of a department or other group will make careful preparation in order to make the most of such sessions by (1) providing needed materials and resources, (2) promoting prompt and regular attendance of the members, (3) seeking to develop a rewarding and inspiring fellowship, (4) encouraging democratic, creative participation on the part of all, and (5) manifesting personal interest, enthusiasm, and devotion. Such program-planning groups will be formed in many different ways, for different age groups and in connection with the various functions of the program. They will naturally lead into the kind of evaluation sessions which will be discussed later.

Working with Functional Groups. As has been indicated, all kinds of groups will be found in a well-rounded program. The supervisor will need to identify any group with which he can undertake serious improvement measures. The functional or commission organization of many churches simply means that there is a committee or commission working on the development and improvement of each of the functions or major ministries the church should provide for the entire constituency. Commissions on worship, study and instruction, recreation and fellowship, missions, stewardship and leadership development are among those frequently set up to make sure that the best possible program is provided in each of these important aspects of church life and work. A committee on worship and the devotional life may well study intensively the worship needs of the total constituency of the church to discover needed improvement. Such a committee will be concerned to make sure that various age groups throughout the church are provided with worship suited to their respective interests and abilities. It will consider also the kinds of devotional training that should be carried forward for these various groups. In many churches worship for the total constituency is provided in a haphazard and piecemeal fashion. There is no serious over-all study of the worship needs of the total constituency and of how best to meet these needs. Often the "worship service of the church," the traditional eleven o'clock service, is planned without reference to the worship that is provided for children and youth in the church-school hour. There is no intelligent decision as to whether these young people should be expected to "attend church." Likewise those who guide the worship experiences of various age groups frequently have little concern for the relation of departmental worship to the preaching worship service.

A church committee should deal continuously and experimentally with such questions as the following:

1. How satisfactory is the form of worship used regularly in the preaching service? What modifications, if any, are desired? In such a consideration the minister of course is the key person and should have a most influential voice in the decisions reached. Yet lay persons are deeply involved in such worship and should be heard. Many services could probably be brought much nearer the needs and tastes of lay people by a discussion in which they have full opportunity to express their frank reactions and desires.

2. What provisions of worship should be made for each age group in the church? This question has to do with the matter of graded worship. Concerning each separate age group the committee should ask what kind of worship will provide the most meaningful, developmental worship experience. Discussion of this question might lead to one of two decisions: (1) that all but the children should share regularly in the preaching-worship service at eleven o'clock, or (2) that the principle of graded worship should be followed throughout, with the recognition that when different age groups worship in their departmental

service, they are in their own "church service." This decision would probably mean that secondary emphasis would be placed upon the attendance of certain age children upon the "church worship service." No general plan can be recommended for most churches apart from local conditions.

3. To what extent is adequate training in the nature of worship, in the materials used, and in the ways one may participate in and contribute to group worship provided? How can this training for all age groups be assured? What encouragement and guidance to personal devotions and worship in the home are provided?

It is therefore highly essential that such a worship committee should study carefully all aspects of the general problem of providing worship and make such recommendations as seem advisable. The committee should be representative of the various groups that will be affected by its recommendations. Certainly youth representatives and those closely in touch with the various children's groups should be members. It is also obvious that this committee should be on the job continuously, evaluating the results of plans adopted and modifying them as experience suggests. It should carry on such experiments as seem advisable and should see to the provision of a library of splendid resource materials on the various age levels.

Promoting Fellowship in the Church. Much the same procedure would be followed in dealing with other important ministries of the church to its people. In the field of fellowship and recreation a committee set up to provide the most meaningful fellowship possible should deal as broadly and basically with the fellowship needs and possibilities for the church as a whole as in the case of worship. Most churches could profit immeasurably by a more careful and thorough consideration of the extent to which vital Christian fellowship is being experienced by *all* the people in the church, young and old. In many churches there are many members, both of long standing and those recently uniting, who for one reason or another are unable to have fellowship easily and fruitfully with others in the church. Too many people are "on the edge" of activities and group life rather than at the "center of things." It may be entirely their own fault. Some people find it difficult to join in activities, to "let themselves go" in relationships and group life in which they long to share. They need thoughtful guidance. Groups often unconsciously tend to be exclusive, to be satisfied with their present membership, and to enjoy doing things just as they always have and "with the same old gang." Those charged with the responsibility of extending the fellowship to *all* people among *all* ages will need (1) to know the local situation well, (2) to study seriously the methods by which barriers that separate individuals and groups can be broken down, (3) to understand how individuals can be helped to enter more naturally and happily into the kind of group experience they need, and (4) to learn how fellowship in the church can be raised to the distinctly Christian level. They should understand that various forms of recreation may contribute to the development of the kinds of fellowship that are desired. A committee and supervisor will find significant opportunities to bring about improvement in the program.

The supervisor should realize that the fellowship among the members of the groups working at the improvement of the program itself often needs to be enriched. The board of Christian education, the workers' conference, the various committees doing long-time or short-time assignments, need to experience the inspiration, fun, and fellowship of working together. These conditions come naturally to characterize some groups. Often it will be necessary for the supervisor to work skillfully to develop a feeling of group solidarity, a sense of common interest and purpose, and a fellowship of endeavor and achievement. It is highly essential that any group maintaining a life together over a period of time come to form a close fellowship. It enables them to work together better, surmount difficulties that inevitably arise in relationships, secure enrichment of personality, and gain inspiration to longer and more sacrificial service. This is a part of the process of achieving group maturity referred to earlier in the chapter. The current emphasis upon "group dynamics" represents an attempt to utilize more effectively these procedures of group relations and activity. There are some profoundly Christian insights and dynamically effective ways of relating individuals to one another in group fellowship and work that are sorely needed in church life today. Ministers and directors of Christian education in particular may well make a serious study of these newer concepts. The supervisor who is sensitive to these values and eager to grow will study seriously the various ways in which group therapy may be utilized to achieve better results in group functioning and to help individuals in making their adjustments to one another. Certainly there will be times of prayer and heart searching as workers endeavor to tap personally the infinite spiritual resources available for personal religious devotion and service.

Dealing with Problems. One of the most natural and frequent ways of improvement to be undertaken is in dealing with the innumerable and inevitable problems that arise in an ongoing program. The supervisor is a "trouble shooter" of a sort. Often a supervisor who has encountered indifference to improvement measures or difficulty in leading a group of workers to evaluate their work has found it possible to make vital contact with a group as a specific problem is encountered and the supervisor's help sought. It may be a matter of poor attendance, unsatisfactory responses from pupils, little outside preparation, a sense of failure, loss of teachers and other workers, criticism of the program or the curriculum, parental indifference, or any number of other difficulties encountered in the work. The supervisor's help is sought. Naturally this constitutes a wide-open opportunity to co-operate with the workers involved. It may lead only to a brief, limited effort to deal with the immediate difficulty. On the other hand the single contact may lead into a serious, long-time effort to bring about a greatly revised program or a totally different method of guiding Christian growth. The supervisor who is concerned for the more thorough discussion of the problem involved will be ready to engage the individual or group in the more basic study of the situation. It may be the beginning of a rich and rewarding personal relation between the supervisor and an individual worker.

A junior-department superintendent who had been somewhat unresponsive to a supervisor's leadership came at the close of a Sunday-morning session complaining of a difficulty in dealing with her teachers' questions. The problems grew out of certain biblical interpretations involved in the lessons they were using. The supervisor could have attempted a quick but limited comment upon the problem. Instead she said, "Miss Radcliffe, the questions you raise relate to problems of biblical interpretation that trouble all of us. I think I have some help for your workers. May I suggest that we meet as a group some evening this week and see what is involved in a serious effort to understand how to deal, not only with this special problem, but with similar issues of biblical interpretation as these may arise in future teaching?" Her manner was so sincere and her desire to be helpful so evident that the departmental superintendent agreed enthusiastically with the suggestion. This contact led not only to one meeting with the teachers but to several, in which the minister was invited to share.

Helping the Individual Through the Group. It is important to note that the group has a significant role to play in developing the individual worker. "Group therapy" is the more technical term used to describe this particular form of person-to-group relation.

The supervisor will hesitate for some reason to make a direct approach to difficulties, especially personality problems, encountered in working with individuals. There may be a lack of rapport or want of confidence between them, or the matter to be dealt with may seem too critical or "touchy" for direct person-to person handling. Suggestions or instructions taken up with the group seem less personal than when discussed with the worker alone. In group discussion the supervisor will seek to handle the matter so that the teacher most involved in the point being treated will take the matter personally. Illustrations may be used that come close to the problems or difficulty of the teacher most involved.

Sometimes it will be wise to discuss "touchy" matters with the group in the hope of securing group support to a proposal to which the supervisor is eager to secure acceptance on the part of the worker most involved. The junior-department superintendent in a certain church insisted on using nondenominational and undesirable lesson material. Discussion of this matter between the supervisor and the superintendent seemed fruitless. The supervisor invited the chairman of the board of Christian education to come to the general workers' conference to give a careful interpretation of the denominational literature and the reasons for the board's decision to use this material throughout the church school. Various teachers in the school voiced their opinions, mostly favorable, and some of the teachers in the junior department welcomed the opportunity to express their desire for at least experimental use of the regular materials for one quarter. Yielding to the interpretation and the urging, the superintendent agreed to a quarter's experimental use of the denominational material. A change in the program was thus made without lessening the loyalty and usefulness of the superintendent. Of course the supervisor made particular effort to assist the superintendent and teachers to understand and make full use of the courses of study and resources associated with them.

Often oversensitiveness or "touchiness" on the part of individuals may be lessened or eliminated when they share in group activity where there is good-natured give and take in criticisms, suggestions, and democratic decisions. It is nearly always safe to appeal to the democratic spirit in the acceptance of majority votes. Action upon the majority decision, however, need not mean that the opinions and feelings of minority groups or individuals are to be treated indifferently. Sometimes it will seem best to postpone action on majority decisions if there is still strong sentiment to the contrary on the part of some members. Human relations are of paramount importance in most working groups in the church. A feeling of fun and fellowship permeating the group will make it more likely that changes can be made without hurting individuals. People regarded as "queer" in some ways, or angular in personal expressions and relationships, or those who find it difficult to "be themselves" or "let themselves go" in the group need frequent opportunities for wholesome group life. In some cases they will need to be left alone to find their way into more desirable and enjoyable relationships; in other instances the supervisor may render significant service to them by seeing that certain contacts are made or activities promoted, or that responsibility and initiative on their part are exercised. How much latent ability, unsuspected talent, and personal resourcefulness have been thus uncovered and made available to individuals and groups, any leader with experience can affirm. One frequently feels keenly that an amazing amount of talent and potential service in the church goes undiscovered and unused because we are not resourceful enough to find and release it.

In a similar manner individual workers may find great encouragement and inspiration in association with the larger group. Frequently teachers and counselors feel quite alone in the discharge of their responsibility. They think they alone face certain difficulties and discouragements. They often get the feeling that their efforts and sacrifices are unappreciated. Certainly too many of them work through long periods with no one being thoughtful enough to express appreciation of their services. Many an individual worker has gained great inspiration for faithful service by sharing in a dedication service for the church-school staff. Some have found encouragement through a session in which generous sharing of experiences revealed the fact that most of the workers had similar difficulties and discouraging moments. Frequently in such meetings an inspiring or helpful speaker has been of immeasurable encouragement.

Training Opportunities. Stress has been laid upon the necessity of providing continuous opportunities for training those engaged in Christian education. Every possible occasion must be used. Much of it will occur in group associations. Classes of one kind or another set up for the specific purpose of affording some kind of group study will probably be the most common form in which such training will be provided. It has also been indicated that considerable training of a very practical nature may be given through the various groups which have been discussed in this chapter. Particularly profitable from the standpoint of growth in understanding and skill are the program-planning and evaluation sessions. This is especially true if those in charge appreciate the value to the participants of discussions that involve principles, methods, and resources related to the programs under consideration. What is of concern to us here is the fact that all group activities have training possibilities, and those in charge should seek to realize these opportunities.

Many groups will be well aware of their problems and eager to deal constructively with them, especially if assistance is available. Others may need considerable guidance in locating and analyzing their problems. For the latter there are various ways in which they may be made more intelligent and sensitive to weaknesses or difficulties in their work. Evaluation schedules that call attention to the full range of items involved in a teaching situation will be found helpful. The less elaborate and exacting forms will need to be used first. Such instruments will serve to sensitize workers to aspects of the program easily overlooked or taken for granted. It will lead often to intelligent self-criticism on their part. In groups that are slow to criticize their work the supervisor may raise carefully prepared questions that call for some kind of evaluation of the activities and relationships engaged in. Usually the supervisor will be ready to report observations or make other comments growing out of his own study of the work being evaluated.

Evaluating the Effectiveness of Christian Education. As has been suggested, a program-planning group inevitably turns at some time to the evaluation of the effectiveness of their work. This may occur on any level from the board of Christian education reviewing the total educational program to the two or three individual workers leading in the activities of some small group. Such evaluation will be carried forward on various levels of thoroughness and skill. It will range from simple inquiries into the response of pupils and the general effectiveness of the materials, activities, and methods of leadership employed to the more exacting forms of testing and measurement. Careful evaluation has in general been lacking in most churches. Workers have usually been giving all they have to the sheer efforts involved in carrying on their given activity. The same lack of educational insights and concern that has contributed to unthinking following of traditional patterns of education has also led workers to be uncritical of their work. In many churches from one year's end to another no one has made careful inquiry into the effectiveness with which the work of the various classes, departments, and other groups is being carried forward.

One of the newer emphases in the program of Christian education is that of evaluation. A better understanding of objectives has led many groups to use the statement of outcomes sought as a simple measure of results. To what extent are the objectives sought being realized? *The clearer and more detailed the objectives are, the better they will serve in evaluation.* Standards for the total program, or for various aspects of it, also provide means of evaluation. Some standards have been developed with a rating scale which calls for an evaluation by those participating in the program of one aspect after another in terms of percentages or a sliding value scale. Evaluation schedules have been developed to guide workers in making a systematic check on the results being achieved or the degree to which the program and methods employed measure up to those proposed in the standards. More exacting evaluation comes in the form of various types of tests. Not many of these have been developed in religious education, and they are usually somewhat difficult of administration and interpretation. Yet they represent a kind of evaluation that must eventually be made. The public schools have made remarkable progress in evaluation and testing, and marked improvement in their work has resulted from the systematic effort to gain knowledge of what they are accomplishing. This aspect of improvement is so important that an entire chapter will be devoted to it.

For Further Study

1. Prepare a statement setting forth your own conception of supervisory guidance through group activity.
2. Canvass your situation to discover the groups that are functioning effectively and those that are failing to work well at their tasks.
3. Indicate how you would go about using such groups in aiding individuals and in improving aspects of the program.
4. How can you further develop your own insights and skills in working with and through groups in supervisory service?

CHAPTER SIX

Guiding Individual Workers

IMPROVEMENT of Christian nurture in the last analysis is a highly individualistic matter. It comes about when the leader working with an individual or a group is able to render the process more effective. Guidance of the individual worker is the *key* to improvement because the individual worker is the *key* to education. We recall again the observation that "the teacher is 90 per cent of the curriculum." If ineffectiveness characterizes the program in any local church, its source will be intimately related to individual workers. The person charged with responsibility for supervision will be concerned to know better how to guide the individual at work in the program. Such leadership will require much insight, skill, and tact for the reason that in religious education the supervisor will be dealing for the most part with volunteer and untrained workers. This fact alone may seem to rule out the possibility of thoroughgoing supervision. The factors in public education that make supervision of individual teachers the common practice do not prevail in Christian education, namely, professionally trained teachers, professionally trained supervisors, adequate time and educational facilities, and the general expectation that such work with individual teachers will go on. Yet supervision of the individual worker must be attempted in Christian education.

Counseling Individual Workers Imperative. Tribute has already been paid to the great army of consecrated volunteer workers in Christian education. No comment or criticism made here should be interpreted as an effort to discount or discourage their use in the local church. The program would be greatly impoverished without the Christian personalities, devoted services, and significant contributions represented in them. The main concern of supervision is not only to make their services more effective but also to create the conditions that will render their work more enjoyable to them. Scores of these workers serve from year to year with a feeling of inadequacy and failure, and many give up their work in the church school for this reason. If the continued services of these lay people can be conserved and if they can be enabled to find greater satisfaction in their work through the aid given them by some helping teacher or supervisor, then one of the major objectives of supervision shall have been accomplished. Any supervisor who can work with people to bring this about will be rendering a major contribution to the program.

Ways of Guiding Individual Workers. Because of the importance of continuous aid being given to individual workers, and also because of the difficulties involved in assisting volunteer teachers, it is necessary for the supervisor to canvass carefully the ways of working with such teachers. Many of the more effective ways of assisting individuals at work have already been suggested. Practically all that has been suggested in connection with group activities has been designed to aid the individual worker. Training classes, workers' conferences, program-planning sessions, reading suggestions, all have as their objective the training of individual workers and the improvement of Christian education. Certain definite procedures which the supervisor will engage in bear more directly upon the work of the individual leader and need detailed consideration. Among these are program-planning sessions, preteaching conferences, observation of leaders at work, follow-up conferences, evaluation procedures, cadet or practice teaching, and directed reading and study. Individual workers, as we are thinking of them here, may be related to practically every aspect of the program of the church: general and departmental superintendents, teachers, youth counselors, recreational leaders, secretarial staff members, workers in men's and women's organizations, visitors, parents, and even the minister himself. Any worker identified in any way with the church program may be helped to do a better job.

Preparing Individuals for Counseling. The success of counseling depends much upon how individual workers are prepared for such assistance. Rapport should be established between the one who is counseling and those with whom he works. The supervisor must avoid creating the impression that he is a "critic teacher," or a "snoopervisor," or an inspector, or a superior worker. Any one of these impressions registered in the mind of the one to be helped blocks the way for effective guidance. There are various ways of establishing right relations at the beginning. Much depends upon how the workers are introduced to the supervisor. Especially will this be true of a professionally trained leader who is brought in from the outside. Usually the employment of such a staff member will grow out of discussions on the part of the various groups of workers in the local church where the needs of such assistance and the kinds of help that may be expected from such a worker will be discussed. Here is a good place for the groundwork of understanding to be laid. Stress the fact that such a worker is being brought into the situation, not to take the place of anyone in the program or to do the work that anyone else can do, but rather to give assistance to all workers in need of help. The more clearly the duties and responsibilities of the director or supervisor are understood by all, the better will be the working relation. This will prevent the confusion and misunderstanding that sometimes prevail when a director of Christian education is employed. Such a staff member should be thought of primarily as a co-worker with all who are engaged in the program in the church.

In the case of the departmental or other leaders within the church serving as supervisor or helping teacher the same approach may be made. Such a worker is there to give assistance in every way possible. The individual worker must be helped to understand that such assistance can be effective only as those who are on the job invite it and co-operate with those who are attempting to serve. If some member of the staff is made supervisor, it may be advisable not to focus attention upon the securing of such supervisory leadership except by helping those at work in the program to understand that assistance is available. Often they will be made aware of such help only as the supervisor quietly and unostentatiously fits into the role of helping teacher. The best possible basis for rapport between supervisor and worker is the realization on the part of the teacher that real help is being given. The best basis for any "authority" of the supervisor is that which comes, not from "official appointment," but from effective service to the working staff. The supervisor should do everything possible to disabuse the minds of those with whom he is working of erroneous conceptions of the supervisory function. Practical insight into human nature and skill in personal relations will be a first requirement of the supervisor in dealing with people.

Getting Acquainted with the Worker. The supervisor will need to know as much as possible about the worker's background of training and experience. Frequently such information is secured as a matter of course, either as one joins the church or as part of a general canvass of leadership possibilities among the members of the church or as he becomes one of the working staff. Many churches have found it advisable to secure full information regarding the previous training and types of service rendered by all who join the staff. In some cases every adult member of the church is asked to fill out a blank form for that purpose. This information aids not only in supervisory work but also in the discovery and placement of workers in the program. Such information often assists the supervisor in recognizing special abilities and needs. A departmental superintendent found herself puzzled over the ineffectiveness of a teacher who was on the staff at the time she became superintendent. Observation convinced her that the teacher possessed ability and had skill. Quietly she inquired into the previous experience and training of the worker. It was discovered that the teacher had at one time served in the public school and that she had taken several courses in a church teacher-training school. Conversation with her revealed also that she had attempted several improvement measures with a previous departmental superintendent only to be rebuffed on each attempt. She had consequently settled into a more or less routine job of teaching her class. The discovery of this background of teaching and experience enabled the supervisor to encourage and assist the teacher to superior performance with her pupils, which not only improved her work but also inspired other teachers in the department to better work.

The alert supervisor may become acquainted with members of the staff through chance conversation, in personal conferences, in staff meetings, and through observation of the worker on the job. In these contacts will be discovered the special abilities and interests, the limitations and weaknesses, of workers, their needs for inspiration, guidance, and the forms of assistance that should be given. Only through alert and careful sifting of these contacts and relationships will the supervisor come to know intimately those with whom he works. This will need to be a continuous process as the work goes on.

Planning Work Together. One of the most natural and effective ways of developing co-operative relations between the supervisor and the individual worker will be in their joint study of the work at hand. It may be a teacher starting a new quarter's course or a youth counselor facing a crisis in the youth fellowship program. A newly elected officer in some organization may seek guidance in working effectively with a staff of officers. A departmental superintendent may ask for assistance in planning for a month's program of worship experiences. A weekday schoolteacher is searching for resource material with which to enrich the course of study. A teacher of an adult class needs coaching in the most elementary aspects of discussion procedure as he begins his teaching career. In the concrete practical situation will be found an unusual opportunity for the helping teacher to initiate and carry forward a continuing process of guidance. The emphasis may center in a careful analysis of the situation, a study of the members of the group, the improvement of the physical conditions affecting the group's response, the handling of the time element, or the kind of assignments and work projects to be attempted with the pupils.

Or the situation may be a matter of more clearly identifying the objectives to be sought, so that both worker and supervisor know definitely what to work toward; or it may be a question of setting up some means of evaluating the progress of the group. Interest may center primarily in a study of individuals in the group, consideration of personality adjustments, or the special needs of a problem youngster. Again, both supervisor and teacher may seek to find suitable resource material for a given course or fellowship program. Plans may be laid for the next session of the group, at which time the helping teacher will be present to give assistance or to observe quietly the response of the pupils. One of the most desirable ways of relieving the teacher of any sense of embarrassment or sensitiveness to observation and criticism may be found in a co-operative session in which both of them consciously set before themselves the ends to be sought and the means of achieving them, and also develop an awareness of special problems and create an expectancy of the outcomes of their joint planning. Some of the keenest satisfactions in such work may come as they note progress and find success crowning their efforts. A sense of fellowship otherwise unattainable may result from their joint recognition of failure in their work and their efforts together to achieve success. If the supervisor plans to visit the teacher at work, it is highly important that plans for the visit be carefully worked out, such as will be suggested later.

The Preteaching Conference. Many of the things just discussed will be taken up in the preteaching session. But in this conference the supervisor will endeavor to deal specifically with the program and problem immediately involved in the situation into which the teacher or leader is going. The immediate objectives may be reviewed, the organization of the lesson material or activities considered, and the uses to be made of available resources determined. Some of the leadership procedures may be discussed, the anticipated reactions of the pupils studied, and plans made for the visitation of the supervisor or helping teacher. Such conferences will be particularly valuable to the beginning teacher or leader, who will probably be in need of considerable assistance. They will be helpful with any leader. Frequently the conference will grow out of a departmental or general staff conference, where program suggestions are made or problems raised concerning which either the supervisor or the individual worker will desire further discussion. Not all of the conferences will necessarily be concerned with the more technical matters of program and teaching procedure. Workers may frequently be in need of inspiration and encouragement. They may be struggling with problems in their own personal religious life. Or the inadequacy of their own training in the use of the Bible or other curriculum content may lead them to seek help. The confession on the part of a junior-department teacher of her own difficulty in interpreting the story of Jonah and the whale to her boys led to a number of conferences on the question of basic attitudes toward and understanding of the Bible. Eventually a series of staff conferences growing out of similar need on the part of many of the teachers was held. The supervisor or helping teacher may well be prepared for almost any kind of problem to be raised in such conferences.

Observing the Teacher at Work. This form of supervisory service is not absolutely essential but in many cases will be highly valuable. Some miscellaneous observations by the supervisor of people as they work at their jobs will naturally occur. Conditions in the average church are quite different from those that obtain in the public schools where visitation of teachers on the job is quite common. Some observation in the church school will be more easily done just because of the limitations that occur there. For instance, where the entire department meets in one room, the superintendent has under her casual observation every teacher at work. Without sharing intimately in the class session she can observe the reaction and participation of the pupils. She can witness some of the teaching activities of the teacher. The actual use of the bulletin and blackboard can be noted. By getting into closer contact with a given class observation can become more thorough. Complete participation should always be preceded by agreement between the two workers.

In case the supervisor plans to observe the teacher or worker during the session, the following factors are important:

1. The worker should know in advance and give consent to the visit.
2. A preteaching conference should be held.
3. The supervisor should learn as much as possible beforehand about the situation to be visited.
4. The supervisor should, if possible, share in the entire session.

5. The supervisor's entrance should be natural and casual, certainly not a disturbing factor.

6. The teacher should prepare the pupils for the supervisor's presence.

7. The part the supervisor will take in the session will depend upon a number of factors; it may range from complete non-participation to taking part as a full member of the group.

8. Schedules covering the items particularly to be observed will be helpful in making full evaluation of the session.

9. Making notes and other written comments should be deferred until the session is over.

10. Only in exceptional cases should the supervisor make teaching suggestions or otherwise intrude in the leadership activities during the session.

11. A follow-up conference should be held with the worker observed as soon as possible after the session.

Schedules of Observation. The trained and experienced supervisor will probably be able to visit the teaching situation without using schedules or report forms. The ability to do this will be the result largely of continued study and observation through which the supervisor has learned what to look for. The inexperienced supervisor will certainly need them. The major value of forms that guide in observation and evaluation is that they make sure that the visitor knows what to look for, and in the case of written records they provide a convenient and permanent form in which to make notes. Frequently these forms may be reviewed by the supervisor and teacher, who together will agree upon the items to be studied carefully. They may constitute part of a cumulative record of teacher growth. Such schedules will be concerned with studying classroom work, worship, fellowship, recreation, service projects, counseling, and any other major activity in the program. In each of these teaching-learning situations a great variety of items will be considered, as a review of the schedules that follow will show. The forms presented here are intended merely to be suggestive of the many more detailed instruments that should be developed as supervisors work in the local church.

A basic pattern may be suggested for practically any type of observation and evaluation of teaching-learning situations in the program of Christian education. The pattern here suggested is one that with some modifications may be used with many different educational activities. It is given here in very abbreviated form. It should of course be amplified at practically every point.

1. Type of activity. Does it belong in a program of Christian education? Does it make a significant contribution to the growth of persons? To the life and experience of the group?

2. Purposes. Are the purposes clearly defined? Are they definitely religious? Are they suitable? Are they reasonably attainable? Are they understood by both leaders and pupils? Are they teacher-determined or pupil-teacher planned—or both?

3. Nature of the group. What about the size? Spread of ages? Basis for grouping? Suitability of objectives and activities? Frequency of meetings? Fellowship and *esprit de corps?*

4. Leadership. How would you estimate general ability and preparedness? Readiness for the immediate activity planned? Skills shown in leadership? Weaknesses manifested? Strong points? Kinds of assistance and training needed? Relation to group as a whole and to individual members? Balance between completely dominating the situation and permitting it to go without sufficient guidance?

5. Procedures used. How could one measure the appropriateness and effectiveness for the objectives, for the nature of the group, and for the activities and materials used? Resourcefulness and creativity manifested? Types of resources employed? Motivations used?

6. Group response. What about the response in general?

Of individuals? Interest, enthusiasm, and co-operation manifested? Nature and extent of member participation? Evidences of pupil mastery, skill, understanding in subject or activity? Lead-on possibilities in class? In further study? In action?

7. Comments, evaluations, suggestions for conference. Manner of presenting them.

The items listed in the foregoing brief analysis should be elaborated and arranged in the form of a schedule of observing a teaching situation. It is kept in a general form here intentionally, with the idea that the adaptation to a particularized teaching situation will be made by the supervisor. It is capable of indefinite elaboration and adaptation.

GENERAL OBSERVATION SCHEDULE FOR GROUP LEADERSHIP

I. *Routine Management*
Readiness of leader ____________________
Handling of early arrivals __________ Late arrivals __________
Use of assistants __________ Handling wraps __________
Recording attendance: Regularity ______ Punctuality ______
Entrance and exit of pupils ____________________
Arrangement and use of equipment ______ Use of time ______
Use and distribution of material __________ Conditions of light and ventilation ____________________
Other items ____________________

II. *The Teacher-Leader*
1. Personal Factors: Manner __________ Appearance __________
Use of voice __________ Use of language __________
Poise and self-control __________ Patience and understanding __ __________ Tact __________ Sense of humor __________
Animation, interest, enthusiasm ____________________
Reserve __________ Rapport with pupils __________
Comment ____________________
2. General Attitudes: Earnestness, sense of responsibility ______
Democratic attitude __________ Authoritarianism __________
Experimentalism, teachableness __________ Co-operation ______
Creativeness and resourcefulness __________ Comments __________
3. Leadership Procedure: Evidence of __________ Purpose ______
Preparation __________ Definite teaching plans __________

Extent to which followed ______
Type of procedure used: Discussion ____ Storytelling ____ Directed conversation _____ Question and answer _____ Directed study _____ Project activity _____ Dramatics _____ Special type _____ Committee work _____ Type of resources used _____ How well used __
Effectiveness in leadership ______
Strong points observed ______
Weak points noted ______
Comments, suggestions ______

III. *Pupil Participation and Response*

1. In class: Full opportunity provided for participation ______
Each pupil encouraged to take part ______
Evidence of interest ______ Participation incidental ______ ______ Planned by leader ______ Directed by pupils ______ ______ Evidences of pupil understanding and enthusiasm ______
Evidences of pupil satisfaction in mastery, skill, achievement _____
Social attitude and co-operation of pupils ______
Degree of fellowship and sharing in the group ______
Methods of aiding shy, reticent members ______
Follow-up work with problem pupils ______

2. In Out-of-class Activities: Nature of outside work ______
Assignments clear and definite ______ Degree of guidance given ______ Suitability of assignments ______
Utilization and follow-up in class ______
Recognition of achievement ______
Individual or group activity suggested ______
Motivation employed ______ Resources suggested ______
Resources made available ______

3. In Life and Conduct: Evidences of attitudes being formed _____
Motives established ______ Forms of conduct observed growing out of teaching situation ______
Services engaged in ______

IV. *Equipment*

Suitability and adequacy of meeting place ______
Equipment provided ______ Effectiveness of use ______
Cleanliness ______ Accessibility ______
Freedom from noise and interruption ______
Ventilation ______ Lighting conditions ______
Comments ______

The Follow-up Conference. The conference following the teaching situation is most important. It is here that most effective guidance can be given. Both the teacher and the supervisor have a body of experience in common to share and discuss. The follow-up conference should be anticipated in the preteaching session. It is here that the conference following the visit by the supervisor should be definitely planned for. It will make for a natural rather than a forced situation. Both participants should come to this meeting with real eagerness and anticipation. They have engaged in an experiment in group leadership. They now come together to consider the outcomes. A number of suggestions will make for the most fruitful session.

1. The conference should occur as soon after the observation as possible. Teaching experience and observation will be fresh in the minds of both parties. Such an early meeting will enable the teacher to make immediate revision in procedure in the light of the supervisor's suggestions. It will enable any long-time plans to be initiated without delay. (The term "teacher" is used here to designate any worker taking part in any aspect of the program.)

2. Both teacher and supervisor should make careful preparation for the conference. It will mean that each will come with carefully reviewed reactions and mature suggestions. The supervisor in particular should make careful preparation. This will mean going over the notes made on the observation, checking back on the plans developed in the preteaching conference, selecting in order of importance the items to be discussed, and planning the constructive measures that will be proposed. Illustrative and resource material should be prepared for consideration.

3. A favorable setting should be provided for the conference. It should be held at a time when there is no undue hurry, at a place where no serious interruptions occur, where needed materials are available, and where comfort and attractiveness in

physical appointments put both parties in a good frame of mind. The supervisor's or teacher's home might be the best place, or the supervisor's office if there is one, or possibly the meeting place of the class or group. In other words, everything possible should be made favorable for a good conference.

4. Both supervisor and teacher should attempt to establish confidence and a good spirit from the beginning. The supervisor should encourage the teacher to report upon and evaluate the session first. It is wise to give the teacher a chance to point out mistakes or weaknesses in procedure before they come from the supervisor. The teacher also should be encouraged to point out aspects of the teaching situation where the outcomes sought were achieved. The supervisor should begin his comments by referring to those aspects that are favorable, commenting on procedures of the session that were well handled and noting the responses and outcomes indicative of successful leadership. Upon the basis of such a beginning the supervisor and teacher may move on to a consideration of the more problematic phases of the situation. The supervisor should make all criticisms and evaluations constructive and corrective rather than to suggest faultfinding and depreciation. It may be wise for him simply to raise questions. If observation is to be effective, there must be an honest effort to face up realistically to shortcomings and failures. The supervisor should seek to establish relationships with the individual teacher where accurate and honest appraisals of leadership can be made and where together they can think their way through difficulties in directing Christian growth.

5. Solutions to teaching problems and measures of improvement should be worked out co-operatively by the two most concerned. Here the constructive attack upon the work will bear fruit. What changes are to be made in teaching procedure, in organization of the curriculum, in directing pupil activity, in making assignments, and in handling matters of routine manage-

ment? Before the postteaching conference has ended, the entire program for the next session may be outlined and plans made in some detail for the changes that will be sought. Co-operative planning for the continuing work of the teacher may be the most natural way to keep the supervisor in close and continuous relationship with the teacher's work, to provide a natural desire on the part of the teacher for repeat visits to the class, and to lead to many other postteaching conferences.

6. At the postteaching conference decision should be made as to further observation by the supervisor. One visit may be enough, or it may represent all the time the supervisor can give to one teacher or leader. Or plans may be made for a series of visits and conferences. The supervisor may recommend that the leader visited enroll in some training class or school for basic training needed.

7. There are times when the conference with the leader observed may be helpfully shared by a larger number of workers, for instance, a departmental staff. Such a group may share vicariously in the discussion of teaching problems, participate in constructive planning, and gain insights from what virtually constitutes a splendid training conference. Such a procedure may be followed only where there is proper rapport between the supervisor and the individual teachers. Such reporting may be done also where the supervisor is discussing the observations of several teachers, which makes the conference less personal in terms of any one teacher's being reported. In some cases the supervisor may not feel free to report in a personal conference to the teacher visited. It may be necessary to bring some of the observations and suggestions into a group meeting where they may seem less personal than they would be in a personal conference. Often much can be accomplished in a group conference with a given individual with whom the supervisor is working who might react unfavorably to direct personal counseling.

Teacher Guidance Through Written Reports. Teacher guidance may be carried on almost wholly through written communication. While not the most fruitful manner of providing assistance, yet in some situations where personal conferences are difficult or impossible, it may be found helpful. The teacher or group leader prepares a teaching plan in writing which is submitted to the supervisor in advance of its actual use. The supervisor reviews it carefully and returns it with comments in time for helpful suggestions to be incorporated in the teaching. Following the class session the teacher sends to the supervisor a detailed report on the classwork, describing what actually happened, adding self-criticism of teaching procedures and personal recommendations for improvement. This report is studied by the supervisor and is returned to the teacher with further suggestions for future leadership. This process of report and guidance may occur as often as both parties have time for it and as they may find it profitable. It can be carried on with workers in any area of the educational program. The supervisor will be considerably handicapped by not observing and conferring personally with the worker. Yet it is a developmental activity for the worker to attempt to describe in writing with as much objectivity as possible the teaching procedure that is followed and to outline constructive plans for improvement.

In some situations a detailed account of what happens in a teaching situation may be desired, yet it is impossible or undesirable for the supervisor to visit the session personally. A tape recorder may be used profitably. The entire proceedings may be reproduced, not once but an indefinite number of times for study. The leader's procedure may be analyzed and the responses of the members of the group evaluated. It is entirely possible that the tape recorder may be used extensively in this connection in the future. It is also possible for an assistant teacher to make extensive notes on a situation being observed.

Continuing Growth for Workers. It is obvious that through all the guidance activities suggested in the foregoing there will be abundant incentive and opportunity for promoting the continuous growth of individual workers. We are concerned not alone with increasing pedagogical skills and knowledge of lesson and resource materials, but also with the teacher's growing understanding of the meaning of the Christian religion for his life and for the lives of those with whom he works. There is perhaps no other form of leadership that requires as much in personal development of him who would be a guide as teaching and working in the Christian Church. One cannot lead others where he himself has not gone. He will need to be on the frontiers of increasing spiritual insight, to move with the "cutting edge" of Christian principles as they apply to social problems, and to strive to extend the reach and richness of the Christian fellowship of which he is a part beyond its present boundaries. Part of such continuing growth will result from the processes of living and working within a dynamic fellowship. Other aspects of such development will come as workers undertake serious guided study of their own religious growth.

For Further Study

1. To what extent do workers in your church need individual guidance? To what degree are they now receiving counseling? By whom is such assistance being given?
2. Identify the workers in your church most in need of supervisory assistance? Indicate those most capable of guiding individual workers.
3. How may such workers be prepared for supervisory guidance?
4. Study the various means of counseling suggested in this chapter, indicating those you consider most appropriate for the various types of workers.
5. If you are a supervisor, outline your own program of supervisory guidance for the next few weeks, identifying the workers to be assisted, methods of working with them, resources to be used, and so on. How may you better equip yourself for such leadership?

CHAPTER SEVEN

Developing Competent Creative Workers

T*RAINED LEADERS the Key to Improvement.* Most of the steps toward improvement in the educational program thus far discussed center in leadership. Unless a local church has plans under way for the continuous development of competent creative workers, it will always be shorthanded in service. Leadership education is an essential undergirding for any effective program of Christian nurture. Many denominations and local churches have never made a statesmanlike approach to the task of training leaders. They have proceeded on the assumption that somehow without advance planning and preparation leaders would be available when they are needed. This has not been the case. Many churches fervently pray for leaders without at the same time doing anything to fulfill the conditions for an answer to their prayer. Scores of churches are compelled to draft people, young and old, upon short notice for leadership they usually are slightly or in no way prepared to render. Church schools have been in existence long enough for each local church to know what leaders will be needed each year. Experience also shows that no matter how well the program is staffed for one year, the turnover in workers each year is high. Many new staff members will be needed each year.

It is estimated that at least two million men and women are serving voluntarily each year in educational work in the local churches of Protestantism. What a mighty army in the service of the Kingdom! How many of them have received some training for this important work? At least half a million new recruits are added to this group each year. What percentage of these new workers come with some measure of training for this difficult work? The average period of volunteer service is between three and four years. This means an annual turnover of from one fourth to one third of the workers. What a task of teacher training rests upon Protestantism! It is to be hoped that as increasing numbers of workers secure training, they will find so much satisfaction and feel under such a real obligation to continue that they will plan to lengthen materially the average period of service. Undoubtedly among the causes for this rapid turnover in personnel are, first, a lack of training and a consequent sense of difficulty and discouragement and, second, the failure of the church to provide assistance through supervisory guidance such as is being discussed in this book. In view of these well-known facts multitudes of local churches are developing forward-looking programs of recruiting and training workers, and many are providing the needed supervisory guidance.

In this chapter the total program of leadership development will be taken up in detail. Many of the aspects of this problem have been discussed in preceding chapters. In considering the over-all picture of leadership development there is no disposition arbitrarily to separate leadership training from the many practical situations in which much of such development takes place. Rather it is the intention to enable those in positions of responsibility—the minister, the superintendent, the director of religious education, and the board of Christian education—to sense the full nature and scope of the leadership problem and review with them the various means at their disposal by which to develop qualified and trained leaders.

Long-range Planning Required. Nothing short of a statesmanlike approach to training workers will suffice. For several decades a well-outlined program for the training of local church workers have been in the making. Various types of training opportunities have emerged. Yet the fact remains that vast numbers of local churches have not developed the plans and made the consistent effort necessary to insure that trained workers will be available in the numbers needed each year for the diversified types of service in the educational program. Nothing short of long-range plans for training workers consistently followed-up will meet the church's continuing need. The program of training may vary from year to year, but always there should be the challenge and opportunity for those willing to take training to get it. Where well-developed plans for training are provided in any church or community, usually there will be found also definite forms of recruitment of leaders.

In one local church as parents brought their children to be baptized, the minister covenanted with them on behalf of the church to take their turn in giving definite service to the program in which they hoped their children would share. This meant of course that training had to be provided for most of these potential workers. Hence the church was obligated to provide annually training for these leaders as their term of service drew near. With this introduction into service, and with training provided which enhanced their satisfaction in activity, many of them continued over a long period in positions of responsibility. Plans such as these represent far-sighted leadership strategy.

In one church that had experienced continuous difficulty in finding enough workers the board of Christian education made a complete listing of the types of service needed in their entire program. This list was printed in an appropriate form with space for individual members of the church to check the services they would be willing to undertake. This form was brought before the entire constituency. While many members failed to volunteer, the net result was a great increase in the number of persons available for many needy places. Some churches use such a form at particular seasons of the church year, in a fall church-wide commitment service, in connection with a "White Gifts for the King" service at Christmas, and in activities related to the Lenten season. Such appeals will be repeated annually or whenever there is need. While most workers will be "hand-picked" on the basis of personal qualifications, experience, training, or some other known factor, much unsuspected ability may be uncovered in this broader appeal. Such activities are usually part of a long-range plan of recruitment.

Challenging Young People. One significant element in the strategy of the church is to place more clearly and consistently before young people the opportunities for "avocational" service in the church. Too many young people come through the years of nurture they receive from the church without considering seriously their obligation to serve others as they have been ministered to. It is true that youth in later adolescence have always constituted one of the most fertile recruiting groups for church-school workers. The effort to enlist these young persons must be intensified. Furthermore the churches must provide many more opportunities of a varied nature to give them incentive to prepare for such volunteer service. Time and again through the splendid means now available the challenge and opportunity for enjoyable and fruitful service should be presented to them. Initial training opportunities will be found in cadet teaching, association with experienced workers, carefully planned observation, classes in camps and summer institutes, service in vacation church schools and the more formal training classes and schools. In a large summer school for church-school workers one church registered twenty-four persons, mostly young people, for two weeks of training with all expenses paid. "We believe," said the pastor, *who came with them,* "that this is one of the best investments we can make in the future leadership of our church. We will not have trained leaders ready for service unless we provide them with advance training." Many churches, if they cannot send a number of young people, select one, two, or three of the most promising youth to receive preparation in such a school or laboratory situation.

A Wide Variety of Talents and Skills Required. Greatly diversified forms of service are called for in the modern program of Christian education. Beside teachers and administrative officers there will be needed youth counselors; those who can lead in worship and can train others; pianists; song leaders for worship, fellowship, and recreation; visitation and follow-up personnel; dramatic coaches; recreational directors; those skilled in handling and using audio-visual equipment and resources; librarians; supply secretaries; family case workers; supervisors; those capable of building and repairing equipment; camp counselors; promotion and publicity workers. Chairmen of important committees, presidents of men's and women's organizations, and similar workers are essential to the church. It is usually something of an "eye opener" to people in the church to discover the wide range of services related to the program of Christian education. Confronted with such an understanding of the opportunities for service, people are more apt to see their own talents in relation to work that needs to be done. It is a well-known fact that a great deal of talent goes undiscovered and unused in many churches. This is due in part to the fact that often those who possess ability do not realize that there is a place for them to serve. It is also due to the fact that such people are not sufficiently motivated to find their place and accept it or prepare for it if need be. There is no substitute for some sort of systematic canvass of the talent, experience, and skill represented in each local church. In most small churches any definite system of locating people who have unused ability may seem utterly unnecessary. "Everybody knows everybody else." Or "everyone with any ability is already assigned to some form of service." And yet only as careful study of the relative importance of the varied tasks and the suitability of different people to handle them is made will the right people be placed in the most needy positions. Various forms have been developed to be used in canvassing the entire constituency to get a record of past training, experience, and preference for work. Suitable cards may be secured from denominational offices. Once instituted, such a plan will mean that as new people join the church, they will fill out such a form, and their abilities and interests will be made known immediately.

Enlistment and Motivation. There is the problem of motivating people to serve. While one of the remarkable things about the traditional Sunday school has been that such large numbers of people have been willing to give their services in Christian education, yet the fact remains that the problem of motivation to service has always been and still is a puzzling one. The chief obligation in Christian discipleship is service to one's God and to his fellow men. Most people will readily admit this truth. Yet ministers, superintendents, and others responsible for securing workers are constantly baffled by the unwillingness of capable people to accept positions of responsibility. The matter of motivation is one that needs careful study. There are various ways of pressing the claims of Christian service. Some motives will appeal to some people and leave others unmoved. Different inducements to service will need to be employed. Motivation may arise out of a sense of Christian discipleship, or a sense of a call from God, or a love of people, or an obligation to serve the church, or a desire to share in Kingdom-building activity, or loyalty to those already serving. The quality of the religious life of the local church is reflected in the ease or difficulty with which lay people are recruited for service. Few things serve better as a "spiritual thermometer" in the church than the number of those within it who see discipleship in terms of sacrificial service.

One important factor in enlisting people is to help them appreciate the vital contribution they may make to individuals, to the church, to the kingdom of God, and to their own lives. If they cannot serve in one way, they may make some other contribution. Some people who may feel that they cannot teach or counsel youth may render splendid service on the board of Christian education. Others lacking in teaching skill may become capable home visitors or secretaries or librarians. Some who lack administrative abilities may thoroughly enjoy working with a class or fellowship group. Persons who like to work with statistics should be given the satisfaction of analyzing and interpreting data for the benefit of others. A worker who would be ill at ease in teaching a class may find satisfaction in directing a group in singing. A prospective youth counselor needs to appreciate some of the keen joys he may experience in helping young people learn how to make religion vital to everyday living. All workers need to appreciate the personal satisfactions that come from such service and the inspiration and fellowship they may enjoy in working with other leaders in the church.

The people we most desire to enlist in service in the church are those most likely to be sought after by many organizations and agencies in both the church and the community. Because of their known abilities, strength of personality, and interest in worthwhile things these people are inevitably engaged in a multitude of activities, most of them thoroughly worthy. But the church must get her full share of the time and ability of such people. Only the alert aggressive church will be able to enlist their services before other organizations have committed them to participation. Only long-time planning and continuous enlistment and training programs will suffice to equip the church with the workers needed. This responsibility rests primarily with the board of Christian education. It will often be found advisable to appoint a special committee on leadership development to care for the items suggested above. Such a committee should have members some of whom serve more than one year in order to provide continuity in planning.

In addition to the committee on leadership development there are others who may serve to discover and enlist workers. The minister because of his wide contacts will be in a key position to discover capable and promising workers, to find those greatly in need of opportunities to participate in activities, and to secure a favorable response from them. He may work directly at this task, or he may act through a committee or other administrative officers. Those intimately related to various aspects of the program will have a keen sense of needed personnel and a personal interest in securing workers. Departmental superintendents will undoubtedly canvass the membership of the church to discover possible workers in their phase of the program. Experienced teachers and counselors may be alert to find young and inexperienced people to become assistants. The superintendent will usually secure the approval of the proper authorities before placing such people in service. Of course any concerned parent or member of the church should be sensitive to the unfilled positions in the educational program and be willing to volunteer or assist in securing someone to serve.

Qualifications of Church Workers. The qualifications that workers should possess are commonly known, at least in a general way. They have been implied throughout in this text and may be stated in various ways. Goals for one's own development are established where there is clear understanding of the qualities of personal life and of the knowledge and skill that should characterize the worker. These qualifications may be grouped in the following ways.

1. Personal religious life and faith. The teacher must have

personal religious experience which he shares and upon which he draws in interpreting religion to others. Few people have this experience in the fullness desired, at least at the beginning. But it should be a growing experience, something that increases as one attempts to share and interpret it to others. Among other things it will consist of the following: (1) consciousness of fellowship with God the Father and with Jesus Christ; (2) personal commitment to the way of life revealed in Jesus Christ; (3) constant endeavor to express this commitment in every phase of personal and social living; (4) recognition of kinship with other people and love and concern for their Christian welfare; (5) recognition of the church as the major agency through which people may be aided in becoming Christian. Ordinarily this involves membership in the church and full participation in its life and worship; (6) eager assumption of responsibility for and participation in the work of the church; (7) willingness to prepare for this work and to give the time and energy necessary for effective service.

2. Knowledge and understanding. There is a vast amount of information which the worker needs. Certainly the minimum to be mentioned would include the following: (1) such an understanding of the Bible and other significant resources as will enable the worker to use them with satisfaction both in personal study and interpretation to others; (2) some knowledge of the development of the Christian Church and of its present program both at home and abroad; (3) understanding of how persons learn and grow in Christian character; (4) thorough acquaintance with the program of Christian education and more detailed knowledge of the curriculum of the age group the worker deals with; (5) knowledge of the methods of individual guidance and group leadership, particularly on the age level with which the teacher works; (6) some understanding of the significant issues in the social, political, industrial, and economic life of our coun-

try and the world, and of the relation of the individual Christian and of the church to these issues.

3. Insights and skills. Personal experience and the kinds of knowledge suggested above should result in abilities and skills in work with people. Among the more important requirements are the following: (1) insights into the interests, needs, problems, and capabilities of the age persons with whom he works—also the ability to deal helpfully with these; (2) skills in sharing with others in the various activities constituting the program, such as worship, study, fellowship, service, in ways that bring about development toward desired goals on the part of all; (3) ability to lead individuals to personal commitment to Christ and to the church and to share fully in its life and work; (4) insights into the problem areas of social life today, awareness of the unfinished tasks of the Kingdom, and skill in engaging with others in study and action as Christians in the community, nation, and world.

Some of the areas of knowledge and skill mentioned above are problematic and exceedingly complicated, such as the issues in the present social situation. It is not easy for any of us to know in exact detail what to believe and, more particularly, what to do. There is no alternative to the necessity of continuous personal study, group discussion, and participation in some forms of social action that we believe are in harmony with our Christian principles. Those who are to lead others certainly need to be as alert and well informed as possible and willing courageously to take an intelligent stand.

There are those qualities of personal life and faith and devotion that are of supreme significance. These almost defy description. There is no simple formula for their development. Most of us have had contact with a few teachers and parents whose lives are so rich and abundant that no one could come in contact with them without gaining something of inspiration and spiritual sustenance. It would seem that the prophet Isaiah had such in mind when he said: "And a man shall be as an hiding place from the wind, and a covert from the tempest; as rivers of water in a dry place, as the shadow of a great rock in a weary land" (Isa. 32:2). We have met them, with iron in their blood, granite in their souls, love in their hearts, and God's sunshine on their faces. They shelter, revive, inspire, and heal those with whom they come in contact. It is as true today as it has always been that there is no more influential factor in the nurture of the individual than association with wise, socially graceful, religiously mature persons. For the church to aid in the development of such persons and to bring them into wholesome association with growing children and youth is to go a long way toward guaranteeing the effectiveness of Christian education.

These qualifications of workers in Christian education, stated in minimum terms, indicate the enormous task confronting the church in training men and women in such understandings and skills that they may become truly effective Christian workers. Such training cannot be confined to any single or simple procedure. It embraces a wide range of continuing activities and relationships and ultimately includes all that affects the Christian's life. The training should develop an adventurous spirit that leads to experimental and creative work. When the leader goes beyond the requirements of the course of study or activity and becomes so immersed in his work that he proceeds on his own initiative to study and experiment, he becomes a creative worker. Those participating in the program should be encouraged and aided to explore the deeper ranges of the spiritual life in personal devotion, Bible study, evangelism, and social action. Fortunate indeed is the church that has a growing number of men and women who are living out on the frontiers of the spiritual life. If such a varied and continuous program of development is carried on in the local church as is here suggested, it is altogether likely that people with ability and training to undertake supervisory leadership will be discovered. *They will simply grow out of the program itself.*

Basic Training Needed. Those in charge of leadership development among the denominations agree upon the kinds of training needed by church workers. One of the best ways to become familiar with the scope of this training is to study the outline of the courses listed in *Courses for Church Workers,* issued jointly by the denominations through the National Council of Churches. The array of courses in the First Series and the Second Series represents several decades of study and experience in analyzing training needs and locating the best ways of meeting them. While other methods of training will be discussed, this outline gives the best over-all interpretation of both basic and specialized preparation for service. The requirements placed upon those who attempt to guide the religious development of others in understanding the Christian religion and its meaning for life are great. Teachers deal with the psychology of growth and learning; methods of guiding growth; the content and interpretation of the Bible; the history and growth of the Christian faith; the organization, program, and mission of the Christian Church; the application of Christian ideals to everyday life and to the social environment in which people live; and the Christian outreach to other peoples. It is the very fact that leadership in Christian education requires such a broad and rich background of understanding that many people, facing such demands, hesitate to assume service. It will be seen how necessary it is for the church to carry forward continuously a strong program of training in which such people may secure basic training. This will be the surest guarantee of improvement in the program of Christian education.

Such training will be provided in a number of ways: sermons, reading, study of lesson guides, discussion groups, and training classes. Every possibility of enlarging the understanding of workers should be canvassed. There can be no letup. New areas will need to be opened up. New leaders will need training. A long-range program of training requires that such courses and opportunities be offered over and over again. Training classes and schools dealing with the subjects referred to above should become a permanent part of the church's yearly program, not just something that occurs spasmodically.

In addition training in special areas of service should be provided. Those who work with children, youth, and adults must come to understand the psychology of the age taught, the curriculum and program to be developed, teaching methods and ways of working with the home. Those who carry administrative, secretarial, or supervisory responsibility likewise need training for such service. The nature of the formal training that may be provided for such service is suggested in the organization of the First Series and Second Series courses referred to above. Courses have been outlined in some detail for practically every form of specialized service in the program of Christian education. Leader's guides are available to aid those who attempt to study or give leadership in such courses. Because of the specialized nature of these areas of training it will be necessary in many situations for churches to unite in some type of co-operative teacher-training program in order to command the services of people capable of giving guidance in the study of specialized fields. One of the primary responsibilities of the supervisor will be that of planning to meet these special needs. This includes study of the background of individual workers, courses they have taken, experience in teaching, the sense of need and expressed desire on the part of teachers and prospective workers. Such a study would include a canvass of the present and possible training activities of the church and community.

Training Possibilities. In providing systematic training both for workers now in service and for those beginning their training the local church will need to canvass a number of possibilities, including the resources of both the local church and the community or larger units of organization in the area. In larger churches it may be entirely possible for one or more classes to be held regularly at various times during the year. Many churches maintain the practice, long employed in church schools, of setting up classes for prospective workers, especially young people, to meet during the church-school hour. In some cases these groups continue throughout the church year. Members are taken through a number of introductory courses in Bible, psychology, Christian faith, teaching methods, and similar subjects. Often in connection with such training the trainees are sent to different departments to observe or to do practice teaching under skilled teachers. It would seem that the least churches could do would be to maintain such forms of continuous training. The local church can challenge its own people to participate and support such activity. It can institute such training whenever it is ready or needs to act, and it can adapt such training to its own particular needs. Where no one local church is able to maintain such a class, it is possible that several churches might co-operate. This would combine the resources of several churches, provide a measure of enthusiasm, and be a part of a larger over-all community program of leadership education.

Other opportunities for offering courses as suggested may occur in connection with a regularly held church or family-night program in which such a class would be a part of a larger program for those who attend. Sunday night also offers in many churches an opportunity for setting up training classes over a given period of time. In larger churches a Sunday-night program embracing various groups might include one or more classes for teacher training. In smaller churches, especially those with limited resources, older youth groups, young adult fellowships, or parents' clubs might well include forms of training as part of their activities. The point being stressed here is that *the church will need to seize upon every opportunity to provide training for those who need it.*

Training Schools and Laboratory Centers. It is becoming increasingly common for communities and other units of denominational and interdenominational organization to set up night schools of teacher training. This movement represents usually a more serious effort to provide a wide range of courses and a more specialized type of training. A community training school held for several weeks may offer several courses on either the First Series or Second Series level. It is often necessary to combine the resources of a number of churches or denominations on an interchurch basis in order to provide highly specialized courses such as age-group training, selected Bible courses, recreation, worship, and supervision. Widespread experience over a period of years indicates the success of such schools. In addition to the training they provide they afford opportunity for fellowship, wider acquaintanceship, and inspiration for all who attend.

The laboratory school is rapidly becoming a significant form of leadership development. Such schools provide opportunity for one, two, or three weeks of intensive training. They combine classwork with observation of experienced leaders with actual groups of children. When held in the summertime they are available to those who could not attend otherwise. They also combine recreational opportunities with the training. It is becoming increasingly common for such schools to be held in local churches and communities where there is keen interest and capable leadership. In some situations they are held over a series of week ends. Sessions may open on Friday afternoon and continue through Saturday with groups of children available for demonstration teaching. In some situations observation occurs in connection with regular Sunday-morning church-school sessions.

Such training brings the opportunity to share in its advantages to those who might not find it possible to command the time and money involved in traveling to a more distant place.

Informal Methods of Training. In most churches there is far more development of workers in informal than in formal training. This is only natural in view of the manner in which most people are enlisted in work and the necessity of using every possible means of giving guidance. One of the most natural means of training is by participation in the ongoing program. One learns to teach by teaching. One masters some of the skills and insights in working with people by being intimately and continuously associated with them. If a teacher takes seriously the responsibility of dealing with lessons of a given quarter with a class of pupils, gives some study to the materials provided, especially the newer teaching manuals, attempts to understand the pupils with whom he works, and strives to bring about development in the areas under consideration, it is almost inevitable that growth will occur in the experience of the worker. Wisely or unwisely, this is the manner in which most teacher development takes place. Unfortunately, if it is not directed and enriched by those who have greater insight, experience, and skill, such training may be unfruitful. Indeed it may result in mistaken notions and undesirable habits of leadership. Those who work alone are apt also to grow discouraged and eventually to give up such work.

One way to insure some measure of training and satisfaction in service on the part of those just beginning their work or who are without training is for them to be associated with a group who are working with the same age and curriculum. Teachers, new and experienced, find association with others engaged in common work inspiring, informing, and helpful. Therefore such association should be provided. Regular workers' conferences may provide such opportunities. Whenever held every effort should be made to render them helpful to the staff. Smaller program-planning meetings have been referred to earlier. This is one of the best forms of training. Where meetings are held frequently, concrete situations are before the group, evaluations of the program are made, and plans are laid out for the immediate future.

The day of the great conventions is doubtless past. Yet there will be occasions when workers within a denomination or in an area of interdenominational work will come together for training and inspirational purposes. Specialist will be brought to such gatherings who will not be available for smaller groups. Exhibits and demonstrations can be provided in such settings. The publicity incident to such a gathering and the short duration of time involved may secure the attendance of local church workers who would not respond to other forms of training. The supervisor will be alert to such opportunities of augmenting the local-church program of training and seek to secure the attendance of workers. It is becoming increasingly a common practice among churches, small and large, to have an associate teacher or counselor for each group in the program. These associates share in the planning sessions, departmental conferences, and general workers' meetings. They are expected to attend the class sessions with the regular teacher or counselor. Through this kind of association and participation they receive invaluable training. Other forms of informal training have been mentioned elsewhere, such as directed reading, correspondence courses, the training gained by full participation in the life and work of the local church, the help received through the regular worship services, and private devotions. Capable and well-rounded workers are not the result of a narrow and limited experience or method of training. Every conceivable form of helping workers will need to be employed.

Guidance in Lesson Helps. An astonishing amount of training is available in the lesson helps now provided with the various curriculums and programs. This is one of the most immediate, practical, and widespread forms of guidance afforded workers in the local church. Most of the denominations have "gone all out" in their effort to place in the hands of those using the lesson and other resource materials assistance of a most practical nature. In teachers' texts, counselors' manuals, and magazines material of immediate helpfulness in dealing with lessons or units of study is to be found. Also there is provided information of a more general nature to develop understanding and provide background for leadership in the proper use of these curriculums. Valuable assistance is thus brought to the worker independently of other forms of training. Everything depends upon the teacher or counselor's awareness of these helps and his disposition to give the time and study necessary for their effective use. Many workers will still need help in dealing with these printed resources. To many of the uninitiated these resources will seem difficult to use. Assistance may be given in the workers' conference, training classes, departmental workers' meetings, and through personal guidance by a helping teacher or supervisor.

Many complaints are heard regarding the difficulty of present-day curriculums. The denominations are developing curriculums that cannot be used effectively by untrained teachers who are unwilling to study and prepare. Denominational boards and editors have faith that workers will increasingly respond to this challenge. Local churches will find available from other sources, especially nondenominational publishing houses, courses of study that boast of the ease with which they can be used. Often such a boast reflects greatly lowered standards of preparation on the part of the teacher and also lessened value to the pupil. In many churches there is a disposition to turn aside from the better and richer courses and programs because of lack of understanding or because of the study they require. The situation can be changed only as the minister, director, or superintendent attempts to give a full interpretation of materials and offers detailed guidance in their use.

Personal Counseling in Teacher Training. All that has been written previously in regard to counseling of individual workers may be regarded as a significant part of teacher training. In the last analysis teacher training must begin with the individual worker, with reference to his stage of development, his special needs, and the practical problems he may be dealing with. While much of the training that will be provided may be of such a nature as to be applicable to all workers, yet it will be necessary to give a great deal of attention to the individual worker. It is for this reason that counseling is such an important part of supervision. It calls for the study of the individual worker's performance, his background of training, the discovery of weaknesses and elements of strength in his work, and his special need of help.

For many workers the personal conference may be the only form of training possible or acceptable. In churches where no formal training seems possible anyone with whom a worker may confer about the problems and program for his group may render highly valuable service. Often the inexperienced teacher will "open up" with a helping teacher whereas in a class or conference of workers he is apt to hold back. Furthermore with such a worker many of the problems of teaching are of a highly personal nature. Individual pupils need study. The particular problems of group leadership need to be analyzed. Aspects of the curriculum being used require interpretation. Plans for improvement must be determined in the light of all these individualized factors. The co-operative study of these matters will lay the basis for the helping teacher to observe class activities or for the supervisor to take over group leadership for purposes of demonstration. Such forms of supervisor assistance are time-consuming and exacting, yet they are among the most effective ways of leadership development and program improvement. Such leadership may be given by the departmental superintendent, the minister, an employed director, or anyone qualified in any sense for such activity.

For Further Study

1. Is there an adequate over-all approach to leadership development in your church? Cite specific facts to support your position.
2. What are the elements of strength in your local leadership situation? What are the most perplexing problems? To what extent is there general awareness of the adverse conditions you have described?
3. What person or group should assume responsibility for over-all planning for leadership development? How may such persons or groups be guided into most effective work?
4. Is there continuous study of all leadership resources and personnel possibilities in your church? What specific plans are followed?
5. To what extent can training needs be met by continuous and effective supervisory guidance of individual workers and small groups?
6. What leadership procedures suggested in this chapter seem best adapted and most promising in your church? How may they be initiated?
7. If you are a supervisor, what are your next steps in directing leadership development in your church?

CHAPTER EIGHT

How Effective Is Christian Education?

THOSE who are engaged in aiding in the religious development of persons are participating in a most important aspect of their growth. We dare believe we are "co-workers with God" in the development of human personality. This is a high and holy mission and a tremendous responsibility. Such an interpretation of the role of Christian education is surely warranted. We are dealing with persons at the highest level of their development. In the inner integrity and dominant loyalty of the individual, in his proper relations to his fellows, and in his response to the Eternal all other aspects of his growth find their ultimate meaning. Because these aspects of growth are so important and in many respects so difficult to deal with, we have been discussing throughout this text the ways in which we may make this process of Christian nurture more effective. We have been concerned with improving *our* part in this co-operative task. We are called upon time and again to ask ourselves just how successful have we been? Can we measure the outcomes of our work? This brings us face to face with the necessity and the possibility of evaluation, tests, and measurement in religious education.

The Significance of Measurement in General Education. Remarkable development in the field of testing has taken place in public education in the last quarter century. Such testing has been responsible in part for much of the marked improvement in the quality of the work done in the public schools. Beginning with quite elementary efforts in this field, leaders in public education have developed measurement into a science and a most important element in the improvement of teaching. Educators have been concerned to eliminate as far as possible ignorance, guesses, and assumptions about the outcomes of schoolwork. They have engaged in costly research, time- and energy-consuming experimentation to discover more accurately how pupils learn, how they comprehend meanings, the nature and extent of their vocabularies at various stages of their development—also to evaluate more carefully many other aspects of education. Through these studies they have developed norms and standards of achievement. A fifth-grade teacher, for instance, knows what to expect of her pupils in the various subjects through a study of the norms that have been established through testing. She knows whether their performance is average or above or below that which should be expected. The larger school systems have departments of research for training personnel who work steadily at the business of creating and using tests and interpreting the data they reveal. Few schools are without fairly reliable information about the mental ability of each student. The I.Q. is part of the standard information obtained regarding every pupil. In more recent years research has been carried on in the field of aspects of personality and the more intangible outcomes of education. Social adjustment, vocational interests and aptitudes, personality traits, and ethical judgments are typical of the aspects of testing now being developed.

Public educators put religious educators to shame in this regard. Those working in Christian education profess to be dealing with *immortal souls of infinite worth in the sight of*

God. Yet their nurture of these "immortal souls" is often characterized by marked carelessness with reference to the information they should have about them and by slovenliness with respect to items of tremendous importance in the development of personality. The public schools do not make such extravagant claims about the infinite worth of individuals, yet their basic concern for the wholesome development of every child in their care bespeaks a sense of the worth of persons that compares favorably with that found in the church or the home or any other institution in society. Every subject and form of activity that enters into the public-school program gains its place there only after critical study and careful experimentation as to its suitability and preference over something else. While these observations are not true of every school, they do represent the direction in which public education has been moving. Public educators have participated in studies of personality development that have been a part of the larger movement embracing psychological research and psychiatric treatment of personality difficulties. All such studies and experimentation may prove invaluable aids to church workers who are sufficiently alert, competent, and genuinely concerned to profit by their findings and procedures.

Can We Test Religious Outcomes? Something of the same concern must come to characterize Christian education. We all too frequently guess, hope, assume, and pray about the desired results of our work without putting forth the effort necessary to make sure that the outcomes we desire are being realized. Our understanding of the learning process has been superficial. Our knowledge of how personality develops is far too scanty. Our disposition to test for results has been wanting, and our instruments and techniques for measurement we have scarcely begun to develop. *In not a single as-*

pect of Christian nurture can it be said that we have established a norm or standard of measurement. The Christian Church has long been marked by a passion to *save souls.* In its evangelistic program the church has put forth extraordinary efforts to bring about the commitment of individuals to Christ and his church. True Christian education is and must be thoroughly evangelistic in aim and outcome. But in the educational approach a much longer process is contemplated, and many more factors enter into the nurture of the individual leading to the full stature of Christian discipleship. A full range of educational procedures is engaged in, normal stages of development are recognized, and a wide spread of activities, materials, and relationships enters into educational evangelism. These aspects of education need to be analyzed into their particulars. In addition to using the methods and materials that lead to their proper direction we need to attempt to determine more accurately just how effective those procedures are in securing desired results.

This means that we will need to press constantly for more objective data regarding the effectiveness of our procedures. Various analytical instruments will encourage more exact thinking. The keeping of records of facts on specific phases of given learning situations will furnish a basis for more careful evaluation and a more reliable analysis of elements of success and failure. More of the evaluative, testing attitude will stimulate workers in Christian education along many lines. E. J. Chave has listed the following values of objective measurement:

1. It may help to break up a situation into more comprehensive parts.
2. It may serve to get more exact data on particular items of the situation.
3. It may help put data in such tabular form that their meaning may be more easily understood and each part seen in perspective.

4. It may give good indices to significant effects of the educational program.
5. It may serve to check hasty judgment.
6. It may uncover weaknesses and permit objective consideration of critical needs.
7. It may stimulate definiteness in objectives and determination to get tangible results.
8. It may call attention to the complex quality of character and the tremendous task of both general and religious education.
9. It may serve to take vague idealism out of some religious education and cause a more thorough study of what is involved.[1]

Difficulties in Testing. Certain questions and problems emerge immediately. It will be recognized that in religious education we do not have a professionally trained personnel. We have the pupils for a very limited amount of time. The investment in time, money, and personnel involved seems to make real testing difficult if not impossible. Furthermore the outcomes we are most concerned with are the most intangible and difficult of measurement. For instance, we should be studying the total personality as it functions in realistic life situations. We can do much by way of observation in this regard, but we have few devices for measuring accurately total personality responses. While we will always necessarily be concerned to identify symptoms and the more superficial reactions of individuals, we should strive to understand more fully and measure more accurately the dynamics of personality. We need to get at the basic motivations of conduct. The ultimate test of any process of Christian nurture is how people think, feel, and act. Yet exact knowledge of how people feel and act is sometimes most difficult to determine. These factors are discouraging and represent serious limitations in any testing program in the church. Yet the situation is

[1] *Supervision of Religious Education* (University of Chicago Press, 1931), p. 42. Used by permission.

by no means hopeless. We will need to begin with what we can safely and helpfully do and proceed further as insights, skills, and instruments become available. We will need to evaluate the results of Christian education on various levels of accuracy and thoroughness. Careful observation of an informal type by various persons identified with the program will constitute the simplest procedure in ascertaining outcomes. Group evaluation will ordinarily be found more reliable than individual judgment. Simpler forms of testing are now being used and can be extended as workers become aware of their values and possibility. The more through measurement procedures will be undertaken by those professionally trained and who work in situations where conditions are somewhat favorable. Directors, ministers of education, and professors in graduate schools of religion are among those who should attempt to experiment in this field. We will need to borrow heavily from the experience and techniques of public education.

What May We Test For? Various forms of measurement indicate the extent and definiteness of the knowledge learned by those we teach. While our concern goes far beyond the information we desire pupils to acquire, yet knowledge is the basis of understanding, attitudes, and action. If individuals are expected to have a mastery of certain portions of the Bible, we should be able to determine the extent to which that mastery has been acquired. This can be done only through some form of testing. That will call first of all for some kind of knowledge test. Then we are vitally concerned to know whether students understand what they come to know. How well do they comprehend what they read or study? Do they develop erroneous ideas? Do they fail to understand the true or full meaning? There is one way to find out. That is to administer some form of comprehension test. Usually such tests as are referred to above take the form of pencil and paper tests, such as the essay, the true-false, the multiple choice, the completion, the simple recall, and the matching test. Such tests are not entirely reliable, for there is the problem of using words that are understood by the one being examined and also the reliability of the interpretation of the answers by the examiner. Yet such tests are indispensible in learning how much our pupils come to know and comprehend.

We are likewise concerned over the attitudes of those we teach. Attitudes are very influential in determining conduct. But can we measure attitudes? Certainly we can make a try at it. We can provide opportunities for people to record just how they feel regarding a person, an issue, or a situation. Such a test might take the form of an opinion ballot, a social distance test, or a judgment scale. Such measuring devices are much more difficult to develop than tests about knowledge. They are not infallible, yet they do give all parties concerned a better means of knowing just how people feel and respond. These various forms of testing render both the teacher and the pupil more curious about results; they raise questions and develop an evaluative attitude toward the activities engaged in; they make for definiteness and exactness in teaching and evaluation.

Leaders have for some time been concerned with teacher-counselor descriptions of personality growth, personal reactions, and characteristics of behavior that indicate needs, problems, and achievements. These items are entered upon forms provided for this purpose or are kept in a semiprivate notebook of the teacher. In some cases the forms used constitute a personality inventory or rating chart and may be used by several teachers in studying the growth of the individual pupil.

Ordinarily such efforts will represent the most thoughtful evaluation the teacher or counselor can make of an individual pupil. Only in the more exacting and professional testing will pupils be subjected to a battery of tests of a more scientific nature. Such tests should of course be administered and interpreted by trained persons. The use of such tests is becoming increasingly common in those groups that make a serious attempt to analyze personality and conduct difficulties. It is altogether likely that such forms of testing will become increasingly common. Steadily but surely we are developing instruments to be used and training research workers qualified to undertake serious investigation. It is interesting to note some of the various devices that are being developed to study, diagnose, measure, and work with personality. The titles of the following instruments, most of them still in an experimental stage, will suggest the kind of efforts being made: Ohio Interest Inventory, Interest-Values Inventory, Social Attitudes Scale, Check List for Determining Attitudes, Pupil Portrait, Personality Growth Book, Ohio Social Acceptance Scale, The Best Thing to Do, A Test of Personality Adjustment, Self-portrait, Mental Health Analysis, Emotional Maturity Scale, Personal Data Blank. In studying these various forms it is clear that we are not ready to use them in the church. They will require more training in administration and evaluation than most church workers now possess. Their value for us lies in the realization of the efforts of this type that are being made and in the suggestion that ultimately we may hope to make greater use of them in Christian education. If leaders in fields other than Christian education are deeply enough concerned over these more significant aspects of personal growth to engage in exacting research to know better how to aid in personality development, how much more should we who regard each individual as of infinite worth in his own right and as a child of God.

Will Pupils Respond to Testing? Many people feel that pupils in the church school will not respond to forms of measurement.

Who knows? Very little testing has been attempted to date. In most cases where testing has been carried on pupils have responded with enthusiasm. They seem eager to know how well they are mastering the material of the curriculum. Students in the public schools have become accustomed to such procedure. Little difficulty in using more tests will be found in the church. Many leaders have discovered also that when properly motivated and in areas where they are particularly interested adults will respond with some enthusiasm to forms of measurement. A minister was brought into a local church to conduct a six-week course on "Using the Bible in Home and Church School." He lacked acquaintanceship with members of the group and felt the necessity of knowing before beginning something of their understanding and attitude toward the Bible. He asked them to fill out the Northwestern University Religious Beliefs Form in which some twenty questions out of fifty-six deal with the Bible. This they were quite willing to do after he had explained his reasons for suggesting it. It called for careful thinking and the expression of their honest belief on a number of critical questions. As a result he had information regarding attitudes of members of the group and where he might well begin in his discussion with them. They in turn were greatly interested to know just how they compared with other members of the group. The whole procedure quickened interest, lifted up problem areas, and afforded a splendid basis for the further work of the course.

It will be felt, of course, that teachers and counselors will not be interested in or capable of administering tests and measurements. Again let us ask: Who knows? Few have been given the opportunity to try. Certainly they can be trained to use the simpler and more objective tests that will be discussed later. As people are added to the staff who are more fully trained to administer and evaluate tests, many workers in the local church can be interested and trained to participate helpfully in such activities. One of the purposes of this discussion is to make known the various types of measurements that may be used in the local church and those that may be used in situations where there are more ample facilities and trained personnel.

Essentials of a Testing Program. Certain things are essential in any situation where measurement is to be undertaken. *First, there must be an awareness of the importance and value of this kind of activity on the part of Christian educators.* Such a concern as has been expressed in the foregoing pages will motivate those who enter this difficult field. It will lead to the willingness of people to secure the training involved and to spend the time and make the effort necessary in this exacting work. *There will be required a studious evaluative attitude toward all that goes on in Christian education.* Such an attitude will keep workers alert to all possible angles of their work. Careful evaluation cannot be carried on without a fair understanding of the bases of character development and the essentials of Christian nurture. Churches must be willing to experiment with different procedures and materials. They must make whatever financial investment will be required. An objective attitude must be maintained toward all aspects of the program so that prejudices and preconceived notions will not prevail over accurate analyses and critical judgment.

Three further things are highly essential: first, clear-cut objectives; second, criteria for determining if these objectives are being attained; and third, adequate tests for measuring accurately the results secured.

The Use of Objectives in Evaluation. The importance of clearly understood objectives in Christian education has been stressed at many points in the foregoing pages. They are particularly important in any effort at measurement. Unless we know exactly what we are striving for, we have scant basis for determining the results of our efforts. The more specific the objects are, the more readily do they serve the purposes of testing. In the more elementary forms of evaluation the objectives will need simply to be put in question form. Some graduated scale of estimating the extent to which they are being realized makes them at least a crude measuring instrument. It is necessary to decide just what information or response is to be secured. Such evaluation scales may be developed for any aspect of the program, such as an instrument the board of Christian education may use to evaluate aspects of the total program or any part of it,[2] as a means of ascertaining the general effectiveness of the curriculum, as a way of determining the growth of teachers, as a check list to study pupil responses or progress, as a device for checking upon the adequacy and suitability of the housing and equipment, as well as serving as a means by which an individual teacher may attempt to learn how well his work in a given course is being understood and mastered by the pupils.

The establishment of specific goals for a department is not now common in church schools. Frequently the literature dealing with a department program includes some statements of objectives. They not only may serve to guide the program activities and emphases, but they also may be converted into measuring instruments of the progress made. There should be more definite objectives for a departmental program and more definite provisions for measuring the progress of individual pupils in achieving them. As a rule pupils do not have any definite knowledge of what will be expected of them. They have little sense of achievement, and when they are pro-

[2] Such an instrument has been developed co-operatively by the denominations: "Improving the Total Program of Your Church: A Guide for Studying and Bettering the Work of Local Churches." It may be secured from the National Council of Churches or from denominational headquarters.

moted, they have no consciousness of "having met the requirements" for advancement. One of the common characteristics of public-school teaching is the fact that usually both teacher and pupils understand the nature and extent of the material, problems, activities to be dealt with, and what will be expected by way of understanding, skill, and mastery, because ordinarily some form of testing will follow the completion of the unit of work. This is especially true of teaching that deals with subject matter and the basic skills. Increasingly public schools and other agencies are attempting to apply these same procedures to other areas of education, such as attitudes, value judgments, personality traits, and vocational aptitudes.

The department program in the church school represents one of the more natural units of organization and activity for measuring outcomes. It is usually a single administrative unit, the pupils do many things together, a definite group of workers is engaged in its leadership, and the curriculum is usually planned on a one-year or three-year basis. The measurement of progress and achievement for a given department program might have to do with any number of items; knowledge of the organization of the books of the Bible, some understanding of the types of literature represented in various sections, skill in locating passages of scripture, appropriate memory knowledge of selected passages, materials and skills indicated in the units of the curriculum for the various grades, development of social attitudes and responses, degrees of participation, leadership responsibilities assumed, and similar outcomes. Such goals will necessarily need to be developed locally in harmony with the kind of program adopted and the abilities of the leaders involved. *Few experiences will be more helpful to workers identified with a given department than to work out together the instruments they will use to test their pupils at the end of a unit of work, year of activity, or three-year departmental program.*

Standard Test Forms. By standard tests is meant those that have been through certain rigid procedures of validation and verification. Criteria of measurement in given areas of evaluation have been established. They have been developed to the point where they are valid. They measure fairly accurately what they are intended to measure. They are reliable because they get the same outcome in the same way whenever used. Standard tests usually have been administered to a sufficiently large number of classes so that norms have been established for given ages or grades. They afford valid bases for comparing the performance of an individual or a group with other individuals and groups. It must be remembered that they are specific instruments, measuring only what they are intended to measure. Most of them operate within a limited field of investigation. Likewise care must be exercised that too much is not inferred from the test results. The interpretation of test data is something that requires understanding and skill. Especially is this true when measurement is attempted in the field of character and personality studies. Usually character tests will measure certain personality factors at a given time and under certain given circumstances. In no sense do they give anything like a complete character analysis. It is possible, however, through a variety of tests, "snapshots of life in given situations," to make an estimate of the actual or probable behavior of an individual in certain aspects of personal behavior. Here again the interpretation of such data assumes great significance.

A survey of the field will reveal a number of test forms that deal with outcomes with which we are concerned in Christian education. The simplest and most reliable doubtless are those that test knowledge, especially information about the Bible. These tests are usually of two types, those testing knowledge and those measuring the degree of comprehension. Most of these tests are general; that is, they test for knowledge and comprehension over general areas and subjects rather than for any given course of study. For instance, the Northwestern University Religious Education Tests,[3] one of the most extended and widely used series yet developed, include three knowledge tests: Series A: No. 1, Life and Teachings of Jesus; No. 2, Old Testament Times and Teachings; No. 3, The Acts and Epistles. In Series B there are three comprehension tests; No. 4, The Life and Teachings of Jesus, Comprehension Test; No. 5, The Old Testament, Comprehension Test; No. 6, The Acts and Epistles, Comprehension Test. These tests all use the multiple-choice form of answer. For instance, from Series A, No. 1, Life and Teachings of Jesus (grades 4-12), the following sample question is taken:

7. When a boy and young man working with Joseph, Jesus learned the occupation:
   _____ of fisherman
   _____ of a keeper of vineyards
   _____ of shepherd
   _____ of carpenter.

The student is instructed to put a check before one answer that he thinks is correct. The comprehension test likewise uses the multiple-choice form. From Series B, No. 4, The Life and Teachings of Jesus, Comprehension Test (grades 5-12), the following sample question is taken:

12. But Jesus said, Suffer the little children, and forbid them not, to come unto me: for to such belongeth the kingdom of heaven. (Matt. 19:14). THIS MEANS

[3] For information about securing these tests, samples or in any quantity, address Religious Education Tests, Garrett Biblical Institute, Evanston, Illinois.

_____1. The Kingdom of heaven belongs to those who have the spirit of a little child.
_____2. Little children should not be forbidden to do what they wish.
_____3. When little children suffer they may come to Jesus.
_____4. All little children must be brought to Jesus.

The student is instructed to place a check before the one statement he thinks is correct. Such tests may be administered to proper groups any time leaders are concerned to know how much and how well pupils have gained knowledge of the Bible, as represented in those portions found in the texts. The results may be compared with test outcomes of other groups. They may serve to diagnose the needs of pupils. They may be used to check the growth in understanding of the same group from year to year. Such tests are representative of a number of measurement devices dealing with knowledge.

The Study of Religious Beliefs. A number of forms have been developed to study the religious ideas of people and the degrees of difficulty they have with various items of belief. These cannot be called tests in the usual sense because for many of the questions asked there is no one authoritative answer unless they are used within the framework of an authoritarian church. Two such forms are included in the Northwestern University series. One is for junior-high-school age and is called "My Ideas About Religion." Some seventy-five questions covering a wide range of ideas are included with the "Yes," "No," and "Uncertain" columns for checking each question. Here are sample questions:

	Yes	No	Not certain
1. Is God as near us anywhere else as in church?			
2. Is God still "speaking" to us today as he did in Bible times?			

	Yes	No	Not certain
6. Does joining the church make it sure that one is saved?			

Another form, designed for older youth and adults, is called "Religious Beliefs." The one answering the fifty-six questions included chooses from among five different categories of beliefs —as illustrated:

	Disbelieve with positive certainty	Disbelieve with moderate certainty	Undecided Not certain	Believe with moderate certainty	Believe with positive certainty
1. Do you believe that God exists?					
6. Do you believe that the idea of evolution is consistent with belief in God as creator?					

Other test forms reveal the difficulties people have in thinking about various religious beliefs. For instance, the test form "Difficulties in Religious Thinking" for older youth and adults lists thirty-five items of belief with the opportunity for the one responding to list the degree of difficulty he experiences with a particular item in the manner suggested in the samples presented here:

	Very great difficulty	Great difficulty	Quite a little difficulty	Very little difficulty	No difficulty at all
3. A sense of conflict between the conclusions of science and the Bible					

	Very great difficulty	Great difficulty	Quite a little difficulty	Very little difficulty	No difficulty at all
4. The fact that Christianity is not unique in having a book whose authority is believed to be founded on divine inspiration					
14. The presence of pain and suffering expressed in war, famine, pestilence, and misfortune, which seems difficult to harmonize with a God who is good					

While such devices as those illustrated here are in no real sense tests, they are diagnostic of difficulties and needs. They provide data on the status of the thinking of those participating, they stimulate further inquiry, and they give guidance in further study with individuals and groups.

Testing Ethical Choices. In such a test form as "My Code," from the Northwestern University Religious Education Test Series, an effort is made to present a spread of life situations common to youth of junior-high grades to which they are asked to give their reactions by checking one of five columns with headings ranging from "Not at all wrong" to "Worst wrong possible." Such conduct situations as the following are included:

	Not at all wrong	Slightly wrong	Considerably wrong	Very wrong	Worst wrong possible
1. Taking things that are not your own whenever you have the chance					
7. Saying that you are older than you are when you apply for a job to earn some spending money					
48. Having an older brother or sister do your homework for you and handing it in as your own					

In the same series is a test form entitled "How I Feel About It" (grades 7-9). The pupil is asked to underscore the word in connection with each situation that best represents how he would feel. Sample situations are as follows:

6. If a player on my team struck the umpire when it was perfectly clear that the umpire had made an unfair decision, I WOULD FEEL
   amused   unconcerned   ashamed   glad

12. If my friend answered back in a pleasant and calm manner when another girl made an especially insulting remark to her, I WOULD FEEL
   disgusted   proud   disappointed   unconcerned.[4]

It will be recognized of course that the responses to such questions and situations are verbal reactions. There can be no guarantee that any youth will act in a real-life situation in conformity with his checks on the test form. Yet much insight may

[4] These samples from the Northwestern University Religious Education Test Series are all used by permission.

be gained into the attitudes and feelings of the youth we are dealing with through such forms. Through experimentation with various tests we may eventually become able to measure with gratifying accuracy the extent to which the outcomes we desire are being achieved.

Testing Devices in Courses of Study. A canvass of current curricular units of various denominations reveals at least an initial effort to include in the teaching plans some form of evaluating results at the close of the study. Also workers are encouraged to develop various measurements of their own. Typical of those tests of a simpler nature to be found in regular courses of study is the following taken from the *Bible and Life Series of the New Judson Graded Course X,* Part 3, for high-school young people, *They Dared to Speak* (pp. 121 ff.).

WHAT DO YOU KNOW ABOUT THE PROPHETS?

	True or false
I. True or False	
1. A prophet is one who has an important message that must get through.	______
2. Amos heard God's call while he was in the temple.	______
3. Elijah ran away from Jezebel to escape the wrath of that wicked woman.	______
4. Amos called the women of his day "contented cows."	______
5. Hosea found out about the unfaithfulness of his wife and loved her no more.	______
6. It was Isaiah who said: "Woe is me! for . . . I am a man of unclean lips, and I dwell in the midst of a people of unclean lips."	______
7. Micah looked for the time when men would beat their swords into plowshares and their spears into pruning hooks.	______
8. Jeremiah was taken to Babylon as a captive.	______

True or false

9. Ezekiel believed that Jehovah was confined to the land of Palestine. ________
10. Job finally admitted that he was a sinner and asked God to forgive him. ________

II. Matching Test

1. Ezekiel	1. The Weeping Prophet
2. Joel	2. The Statesman Prophet
3. Isaiah	3. The Herdsman from Tekoa
4. Hosea	4. The Father of Speculation
5. Habakkuk	5. Prophet of Peace
6. Malachi	6. Saw wheels with wheels
7. Jeremiah	7. Hater of Nineveh
8. Amos	8. Drew lessons from locusts
9. Jonah	9. Condemned the offering of blind cattle
10. Micah	10. His wife was unfaithful

III. General Questions

1. What are the sins the prophets found in Israel and condemned?
2. How do these compare with America today?
3. Give a brief word picture of the following prophets: Elijah, Elisha, Zephaniah.
4. List some outstanding historical events that took place during the prophetic period.
5. Which prophet do you like best and why?

IV. Give five lessons which you have learned from your study of the prophets.[5]

In the unit "How It All Began" in the *New Judson Graded Course X,* Part 1, for senior-high-school young people will be found a variety of test forms: completion, true-false, yes or no, matching, multiple choice, and essay tests; also value scales,

[5] Used by permission of the Division of Christian Publications of the Board of Education and Publication of the American Baptist Convention.

attitude and personal achievement evaluation forms, are provided. Most of these are very simple and elementary tests. But the fact remains that incentive and opportunity are afforded both pupil and teacher to know with greater definiteness what has been learned, how well it is understood, how pupils feel about certain issues and groups, what their sense of values is, and what they propose to do about some of the problems they have discussed. Such evaluations cannot help but arouse curiosity, stimulate inquiry, and provide a more exact knowledge of the outcomes of the program being carried on.

In the *Guidebook to Your Bible,* Course VII, Part 1, The Graded Press, will be found the following simple true-false test. Sample statements are presented here.

WHAT DO YOU KNOW ABOUT THE BIBLE?

(A test to be used at the beginning of the quarter)

You have been studying the Bible in church school and other places for several years. Perhaps you would like to test yourself to find out how much you remember from your former study.

The following statements about the Bible and its contents are either true or false. Read each statement carefully. If you know that it is true, mark T in the parentheses following it. If you know that it is false, mark F in this space. Work carefully. Do not guess.

Example: All Bibles are exactly alike in every way. (F)

1. The Bible has been in existence only about five hundred years. ( )
2. The Bible, as we now have it, is a translation from other languages. ( )
4. Centuries ago the Bible was unknown by the common people because it was written in Latin. ( )
5. Moses wrote most of the books of the Old Testament. ( )
8. We should look for the Beatitudes in the Old Testament. ( )
10. To find The Sermon on the Mount we should turn to the Old Testament. ( )

17. We need to study the Old Testament to learn how people first thought about God. ( )
27. The Bible, or parts of it, has been translated into more than a thousand languages and dialects. ( )[6]

Probably the most significant forms of studying the development of pupils are those ordinary workers in the program can use and in which they can easily be given training. We refer to actual observation of behavior. So many of the aspects of conduct and personality development we desire to measure are best evaluated in close relation to the situations that call them forth. They cannot successfully be isolated from life and measured by paper tests. In such observation great care should be exercised in recording actual reactions and responses. There is no magic in such data. But if they are recorded in some written form, they may be compared with the observations of others. Such comparisons will help correct excessive subjectivity and prejudiced evaluations. While test forms serve to break conduct down into specific elements and provide devices for scoring, nothing can take the place of firsthand information gained through extended observation of life situations, visitation, and detailed descriptive records of behavior. Even if other forms of testing are used, the results obtained require such a descriptive background for the most meaningful interpretation. Is there any worker in the educational program who cannot be trained to make careful and sustained observation of pupils, to visit them and otherwise to keep in close personal contact with those placed in his care? It will require as much as anything else sheer dogged perseverance to stay at the serious study of individuals long enough to gain clear insights into their interests, needs, problems, and growth possibilities.

Christian Experience the Final Goal. In the last analysis it is what people experience that constitutes Christian life and growth In planning programs, in exercising forms of leadership, and in evaluating outcomes our ultimate concern is that individuals enter into desirable experiences. We provide worship in order to make more readily possible experiences of God-awareness. We guide them in studying the Bible that they may more truly experience its inspiration and help. We plan social-action programs so that individuals will actually experience different attitudes, appreciations, and the satisfactions of "doing something about it." We give them opportunity to play together, exercise leadership, and acquire skills which in the end are experiences that constitute growth. The final test of all that we do as teachers and leaders is that people enter into experiences that actually change their lives, that steadily and surely they increase "in wisdom and in stature, and in favor with God and man."

For Further Study

1. To what degree are (1) you and (2) your associates committed to the possibility and necessity for measuring the outcomes of Christian education?
2. How would you proceed to arouse more concern over evaluation and tests?
3. What person in your program may best be trained for this type of work?
4. Outline the more immediate and simpler procedures that may be followed to institute more thorough evaluation of (1) the total program and (2) specific aspects of Christian education.

SELECTED BIBLIOGRAPHY

Practically the entire body of literature dealing with modern Christian education has significance for supervision. As we have seen, improvement is concerned with objectives, Bible, theology, program building, curriculum, methodology, psychology, organization, leadership, housing and equipment, measurement, and all other aspects of the church's program of religious education. It is inadvisable to attempt to list here the full range of materials pertinent to supervision. It will be helpful for supervisors to become thoroughly acquainted with several of the carefully compiled bibliographies that are available. One such is found in Lotz, *Orientation in Religious Education,* pp. 568-83. *Christian Education Bibliography,* 1952, published by the National Council of Churches of Christ in the U.S.A., is especially helpful. It doubtless will be revised periodically. *The Program of Leadership Education, the First and Second Series,* as released through the National Council of Churches and the various denominational headquarters, constitutes one of the best classified bibliographies available. It should be constantly available to supervisors and staff members.

A few of the most significant books and pamphlets in various aspects of Christian education are listed here. The alert supervisor will be constantly on the lookout for material that will increase his understanding and skill in supervisory leadership.

Books

Chave, E. J. *Supervision of Religious Education.* University of Chicago Press, 1931.

Conover, E. M. *The Church, School and Parish House Building.* Chicago: International Council of Religious Education, 1949.

Selected Bibliography

Dale, Edgar. *Audio-Visual Methods in Teaching.* New York: Dryden Press, 1946.

Dimock, H. S., and Trecker, H. B. *Supervision of Group Work and Recreation.* New York: Association Press, 1949.

Eakin, Mildred, and Eakin, Frank. *The Church-School Teacher's Job.* New York: Macmillan Co., 1949.

Elliott, H. S. *Can Religious Education Be Christian?* New York: Macmillan Co., 1940.

Gwynn, Price H. *Leadership Education in the Local Church.* Philadelphia: Westminster Press, 1952.

Haiman, Franklin S. *Group Leadership and Democratic Action.* Boston: Houghton Mifflin Co., 1951.

Harner, N. C. *The Educational Work of the Church.* New York and Nashville: Abingdon-Cokesbury Press, 1939.

Heim, R. D. *Leading a Sunday Church School.* Philadelphia: Muhlenberg Press, 1950.

Lindhorst, F. A. *The Minister Teaches Religion.* New York and Nashville: Abingdon-Cokesbury Press, 1945.

Lobingier, J. L. *The Better Church School.* Boston: Pilgrim Press, 1952.

Lotz, Philip Henry. *Orientation in Religious Education.* New York and Nashville: Abingdon-Cokesbury Press, 1950.

McKibben, Frank M. *Christian Education Through the Church.* New York and Nashville: Abingdon-Cokesbury Press, 1947.

———. *Improving Religious Education Through Supervision.* New York and Nashville: Abingdon-Cokesbury Press, 1931.

———. *Improving Your Teaching.* Philadelphia: Judson Press, 1934.

McLester, Frances C. *Teaching in the Church School.* New York and Nashville: Abingdon-Cokesbury Press, 1940.

Miller, R. C. *The Clue to Christian Education.* New York: Charles Scribner's Sons, 1950.

Powell, R. R. *Improving Your Church School.* New York and Nashville: Abingdon-Cokesbury Press, 1949.

Tower, H. E. *Church Use of Audio-Visuals.* New York and Nashville: Abingdon-Cokesbury Press, 1951.

Vieth, P. H. *The Church and Christian Education.* St. Louis: Bethany Press, 1947.

PAMPHLETS

The Local Church Director of Christian Education. L-556.

The International Standard for the Sunday Church School (revised 1951).

Improving the Total Program of Your Church: A Guide for Studying and Bettering the Work of Local Churches (revised 1951).

And Gladly Serve

The Standard Leadership Curriculum: First Series Courses, Bulletin 501; Second Series Courses, Bulletin 502

(These pamphlets are available through the office of the Division of Christian Education of the National Council of Churches of Christ in the U.S.A., and through practically all of the denominational publishing houses and educational offices. Most denominations publish annually or periodically lists of pamphlet materials of a most useful nature.)